AUSTRALIAN HOMESCHOOLING SERIES

T0359267

Learning Multiplication 2

2nd IN A SERIES OF 2

Years 2–6

Written by Carmel Musumeci

CORONEOS PUBLICATIONS

Item No 502

Coroneos Publications
2/195 Prospect Highway
PO Box 2
Seven Hills NSW 2147

Postal Address:
PO Box 2
Seven Hills NSW 2147

Website:
www.coroneos.com.au or www.basicskillsseries.com

Email: coroneospublications@westnet.com.au

Item # 502
Learning Multiplication 2
by Carmel Musumeci
First published 2008

ISBN: 978-1-86294-216-5

Learning Multiplication!

Hello!

In our **Learning Multiplication Book 2**, we are going to learn our

4, 8, 12, 7 and 11 Times Tables.

In **Book 1** you would have learnt your

2, 5, 10, 3 ,6 and 9 Times Tables.

You will need an Exercise Book to write out your Times Tables,
a sharpened pencil, a rubber and a ruler.
Use the pencil and a ruler to rule up some columns in your
Exercise Book and write out the Multiplication Tables twice each day as instructed on the page.

On the next page, you can colour in the tables on the Tables Chart after you have learnt them, so that you can see how well you are progressing!

Your parent or teacher may wish to reward your good work with some stickers.

By doing these activities and writing each table out 2 times a day in your Exercise Book, you will find that you will soon have them all learnt and coloured in!

<u>Note to Parent/Teacher:</u>
On Pages 59 - 61, there are **Learning Multiplication Ideas**, which may help students learn multiplication tables with a little fun, through suggested activities.

I learnt lots of tables in Book 1,
Now it won't take me
long to learn all the rest!

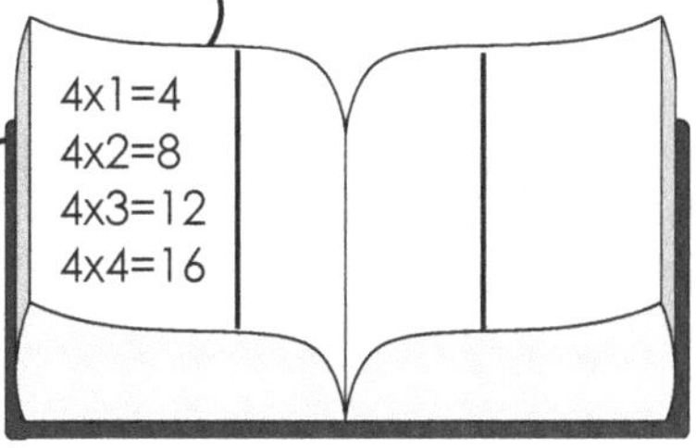
4x1=4
4x2=8
4x3=12
4x4=16

Written by Carmel Musumeci
(for you Esta Jana!)

Times Tables that I have Learnt:

	4	Four	Times	**4**	
4 x 1 = 4	**4 x 2 = 8**	**4 x 3 = 12**	**4 x 4 = 16**	**4 x 5 = 20**	**4 x 6 = 24**
4 x 7 = 28	**4 x 8 = 32**	**4 x 9 = 36**	**4 x 10 = 40**	**4 x 11 = 44**	**4 x 12 = 48**
	8	Eight	Times	**8**	
8 x 1 = 8	**8 x 2 = 16**	**8 x 3 = 24**	**8 x 4 = 32**	**8 x 5 = 40**	**8 x 6 = 48**
8 x 7 = 56	**8 x 8 = 64**	**8 x 9 = 72**	**8 x 10 = 80**	**8 x 11 = 88**	**8 x 12 = 96**
	12	Twelve	Times	**12**	
12 x 1 = 12	**12 x 2 = 24**	**12 x 3 = 36**	**12 x 4 = 48**	**12 x 5 = 60**	**12 x 6 = 72**
12 x 7 = 84	**12 x 8 = 96**	**12 x 9 = 108**	**12 x 10 = 120**	**12 x 11 = 132**	**12 x 12 = 144**
	7	Seven	Times	**7**	
7 x 1 = 7	**7 x 2 = 14**	**7 x 3 = 21**	**7 x 4 = 28**	**7 x 5 = 35**	**7 x 6 = 42**
7 x 7 = 49	**7 x 8 = 56**	**7 x 9 = 63**	**7 x 10 = 70**	**7 x 11 = 77**	**10 x 12 = 120**
	11	Eleven	Times	**11**	
11 x 1 =11	**11 x 2 = 22**	**11 x 3 = 33**	**11 x 4 = 44**	**11 x 5 = 55**	**11 x 6 = 66**
11 x 7 = 77	**11 x 8 = 88**	**11 x 9 = 99**	**11 x 10 = 110**	**11 x 11 = 121**	**11 x 12 = 132**

Colour in the Times Tables that you know!

The Four Times Multiplication Table

4

1 x 4 = 4	7 x 4 = 21
2 x 4 = 8	8 x 4 = 32
3 x 4 = 12	9 x 4 = 36
4 x 4 = 16	10x 4 = 40
5 x 4 = 20	11x 4 = 44
6 x 4 = 24	12x 4 = 48

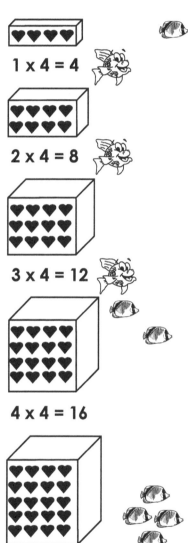

1 x 4 = 4

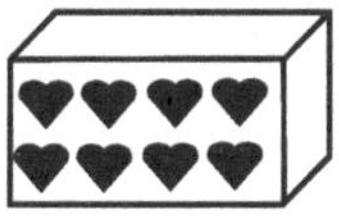

2 x 4 = 8

3 x 4 = 12

4 x 4 = 16

5 x 4 = 20

6 x 4 = 24

7 x 4 = 28

8 x 4 = 32

9 x 4 = 36

Next to some of the Times Tables there is a happy fish.
Colour it in.
You already know these tables! There are 5 to learn!

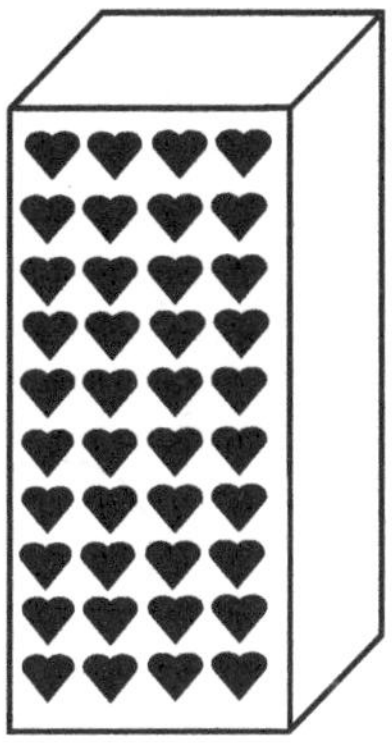

10 x 4 = 40

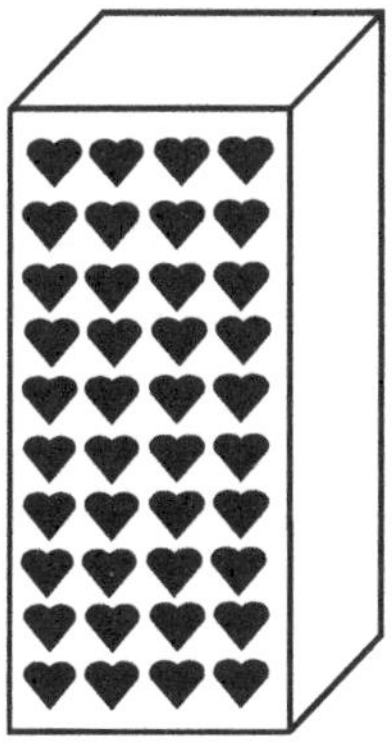

11 x 4 = 44

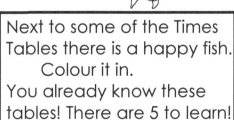

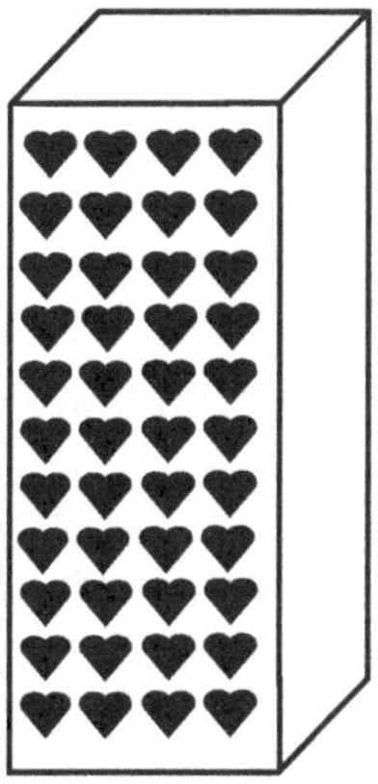

12 x 4 = 48

Multiplication by 4

Write out the four times multiplication table twice.

3 x 4 = ☐   7 x 4 = ☐   5 x 4 = ☐   11 x 4 = ☐

8 x 4 = ☐   12 x 4 = ☐   2 x 4 = ☐   10 x 4 = ☐

4 x 4 = ☐   9 x 4 = ☐   6 x 4 = ☐   1 x 4 = ☐

  x 4 / 32

x 4 / 12

x 4 / 36

x 4 / 8

x 4 / 28

  x 4 / 44

x 4 / 20

x 4 / 48

x 4 / 16

x 4 / 24

R O A R

4 x 4 =   9 x 4 =   7 x 4 =   11 x 4 =   6 x 4 =   5 x 4 =   8 x 4 =   10 x 4 =   12 x 4 =

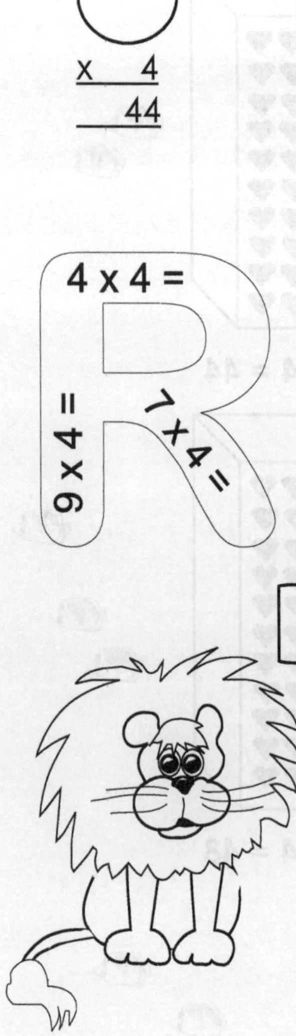

How fast can you claw through these?

2 x 12 =....   4 x 6 =....   7 x 5 =....   12 x 3 =....

8 x 6 =....   3 x 9 =....   6 x 6 =....   8 x 9 =....

2 x 10 =....   12 x 5 =....   8 x 3 =....   9 x 7 =....

4 x 4 =....   5 x 8 =....   6 x 12 =....   7 x 6 =....

Multiplication by 4

Write out the four times multiplication table twice.

Solve the tables, then colour-in with the correct colour for the answer.

3 x 4 =	yellow	8 x 4 =	purple
4 x 4 =	green	9 x 4 =	pink
5 x 4 =	black	10 x 4 =	brown
6 x 4 =	orange	11 x 4 =	red
7 x 4 =	light blue	12 x 4 =	dark blue

Multiplication by 4

Write out the four times multiplication table twice.

2 x 4 =	6 x 4 =	4 x 4 =	11 x 4 =	3 x 4 =	7 x 4 =
5 x 4 =	8 x 4 =	12 x 4 =	9 x 4 =	1 x 4 =	10 x 4 =

What is as big as an elephant, but doesn't weigh anything?

An elephant's shadow.

How fast can these be done?

3 x 9	6 x 6	8 x 5	5 x 12	9 x 10	12 x 3
4 x 6	7 x 9			11 x 10	10 x 12
5 x 9	10 x 10	8 x 6		2 x 6	12 x 9

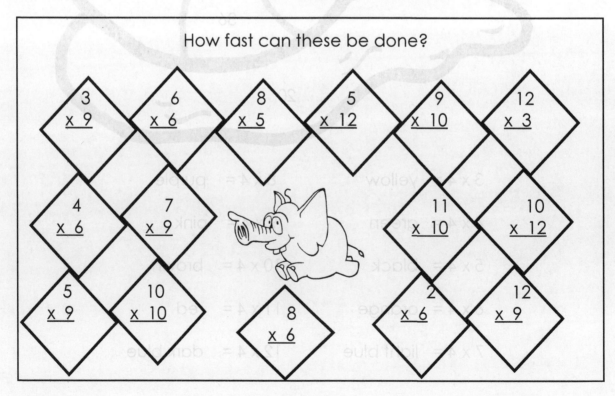

Multiplication by 4

Write out the four times multiplication table twice.

4 x 4 = ...   7 x 4 = ...   3 x 4 = ...

8 x 4 = ...   5 x 4 = ...   9 x 4 = ...

2 x 4 = ...   10 x 4 = ...   6 x 4 = ...

11 x 4 = ...   5 x 4 = ...   12 x 4 = ...

Times the number beside the lily pad by **4**.

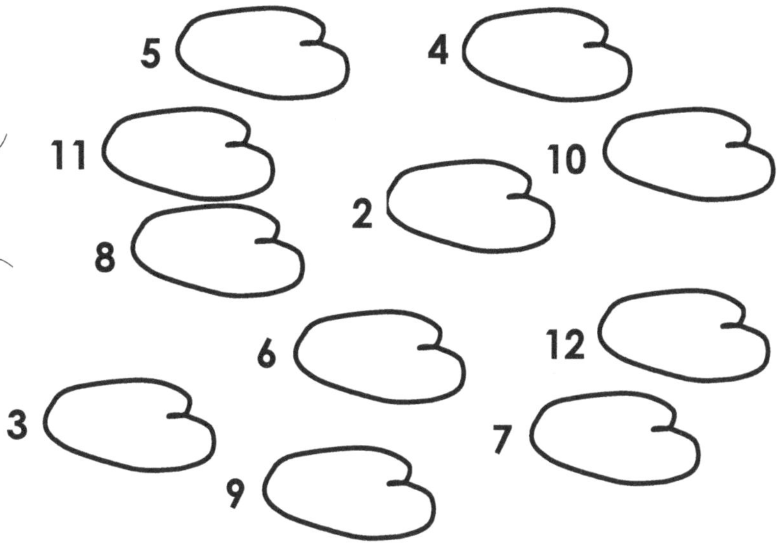

A frogs has 4 legs.
1 group of **4** legs equals **4**.

1 x 4 = 4

____ groups of 4 legs equals 20?   ____ groups of 4 legs equals 12?

____ groups of 4 legs equals 36?   ____ groups of 4 legs equals 48?

____ groups of 4 legs equals 40?   ____ groups of 4 legs equals 32?

____ groups of 4 legs equals 24?   ____ groups of 4 legs equals 28?

____ groups of 4 legs equals 44?

Multiplication by 4

Write out the four times multiplication table twice.

Do you know why the grizzly bear caught a cold?

He went outside with his **bear** feet!

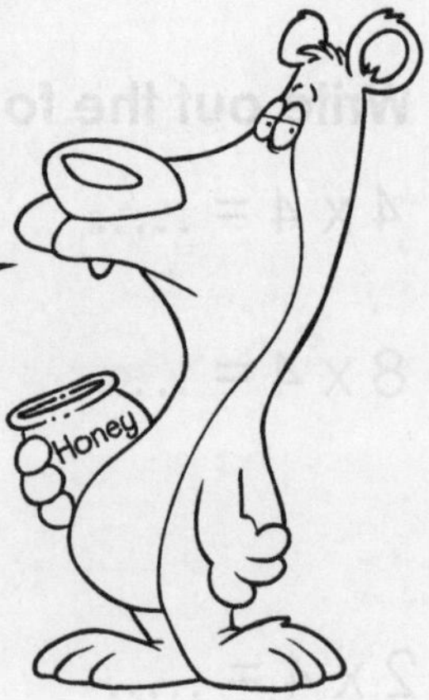

4 x 5 =   4 x 7 =   4 x 11 =

4 x 12 =   4 x 8 =   4 x 6 =

4 x 9 =   4 x 3 =   4 x 4 =

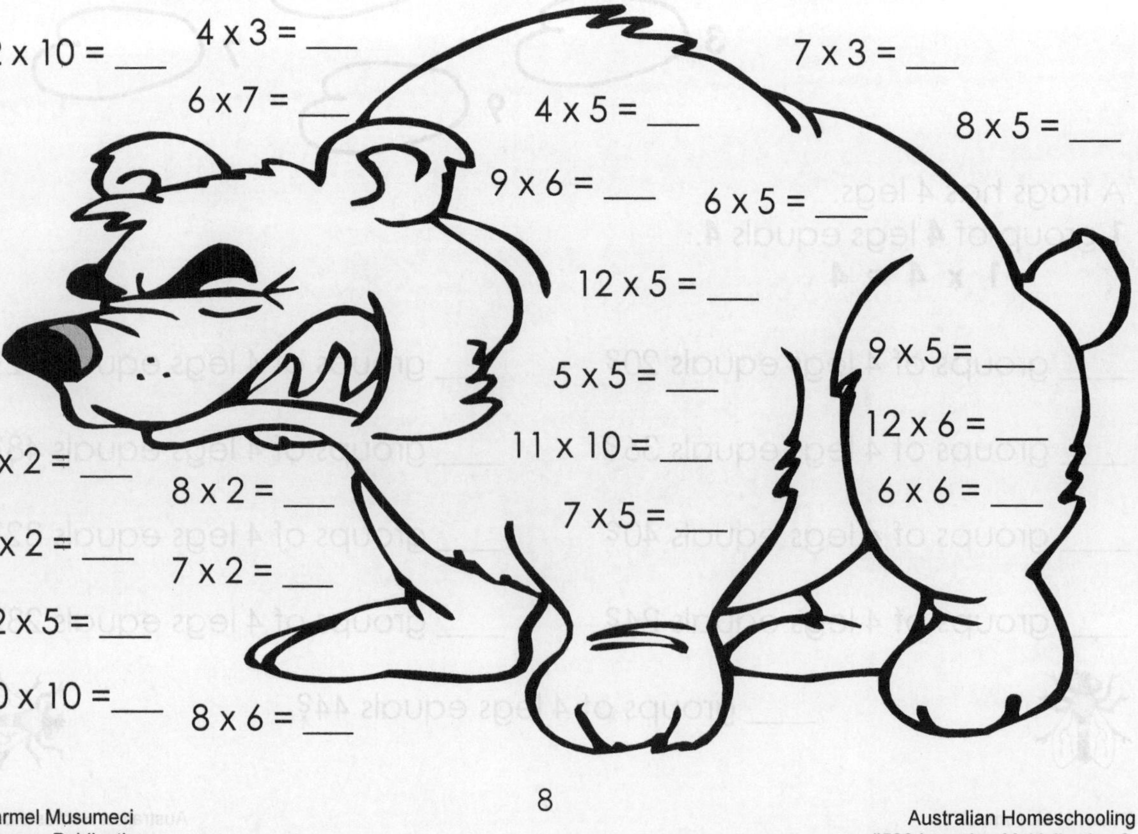

12 x 10 = ___   4 x 3 = ___   7 x 3 = ___

6 x 7 = ___   4 x 5 = ___   8 x 5 = ___

9 x 6 = ___   6 x 5 = ___

12 x 5 = ___

9 x 5 = ___

5 x 5 = ___

12 x 6 = ___

9 x 2 = ___   11 x 10 = ___

8 x 2 = ___   6 x 6 = ___

7 x 5 =

6 x 2 = ___

7 x 2 = ___

12 x 5 = ___

10 x 10 = ___   8 x 6 = ___

Multiplication by 4

Write out the four times multiplication table twice.

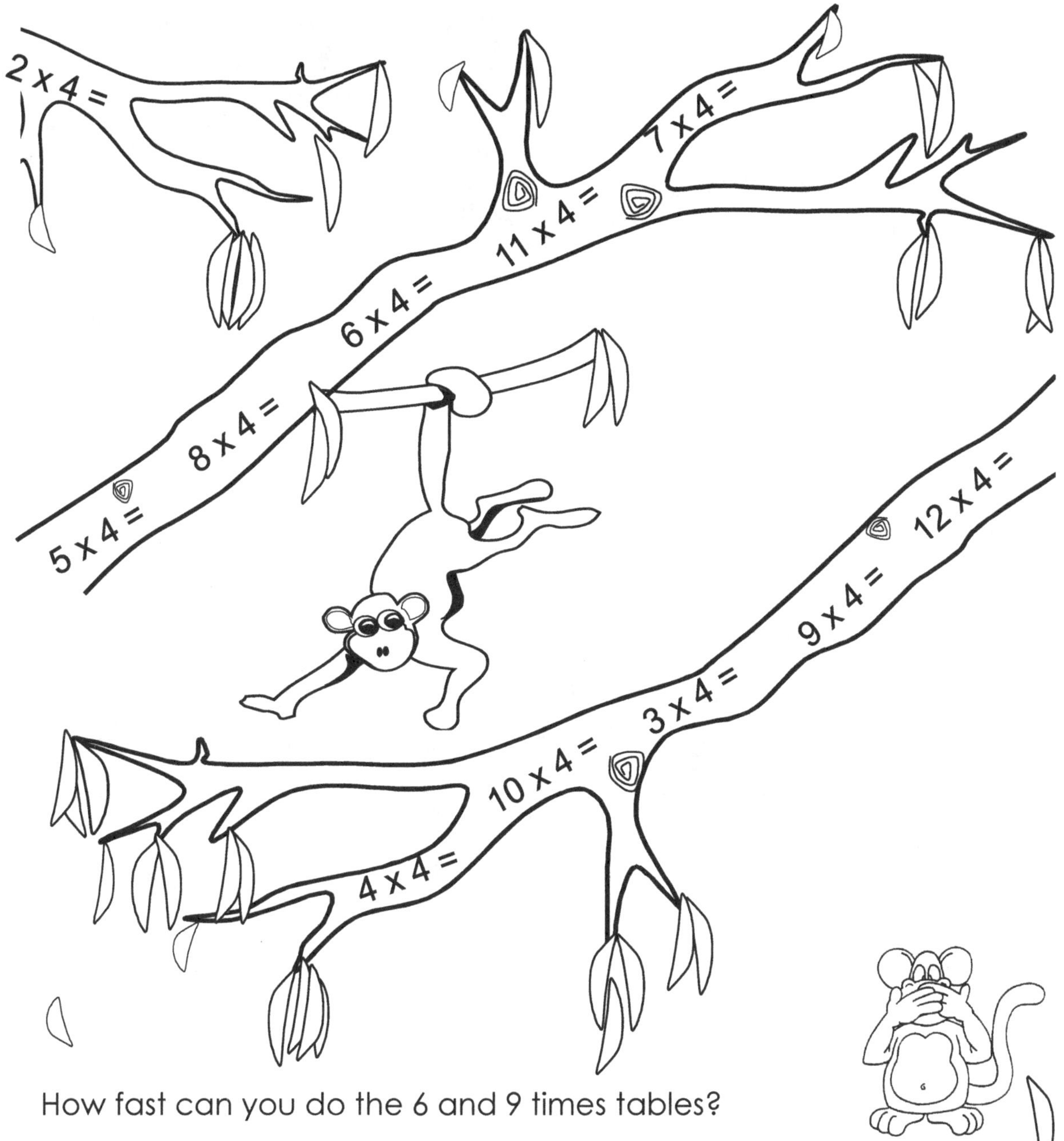

How fast can you do the 6 and 9 times tables?

2 x 6 = ◯ 3 x 6 = ◯ 4 x 6 = ◯ 5 x 6 = ◯ 6 x 6 = ◯

7 x 6 = ◯ 8 x 6 = ◯ 9 x 6 = ◯ 10 x 6 = ◯ 11 x 6 = ◯

12 x 6 = ◯ 2 x 9 = ◯ 3 x 9 = ◯ 4 x 9 = ◯ 5 x 9 = ◯

6 x 9 = ◯ 7 x 9 = ◯ 8 x 9 = ◯ 9 x 9 = ◯ 10 x 9 = ◯

11 x 9 = ◯ 12 x 9 = ◯

Multiplication by 4

Write out the four times multiplication table twice.

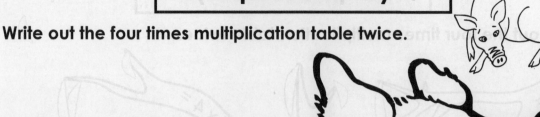

4 x 3
4 x 5
4 x 7
4 x 9
4 x 11
4 x 4
4 x 6
4 x 8
4 x 10
4 x 12
If pigs skin makes good shoes, what can you make from banana skins?
Slippers!

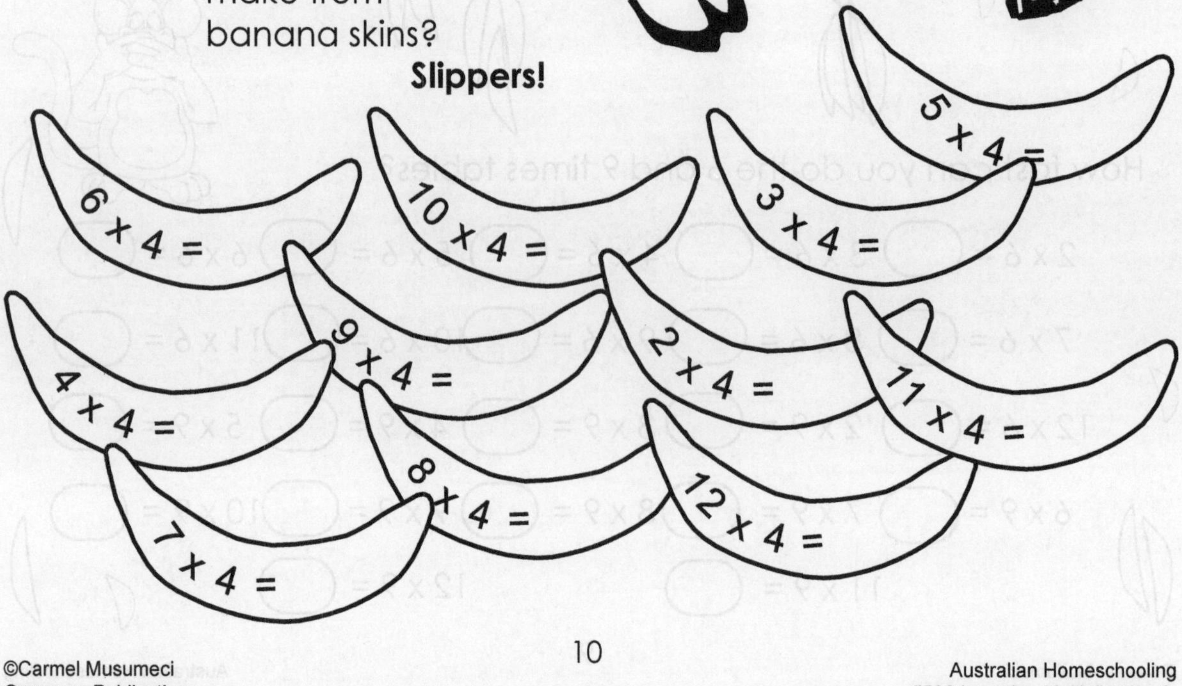

5 x 4 =
6 x 4 =
10 x 4 =
3 x 4 =
9 x 4 =
2 x 4 =
4 x 4 =
11 x 4 =
8 x 4 =
12 x 4 =
7 x 4 =

Multiplication by 4

Write out the four times multiplication table twice.

1 x 4 = **2 x 4 =**

3 x 4 = **4 x 4 =**

5 x 4 = **6 x 4 =** **7 x 4 =** **8 x 4 =**

9 x 4 = **10 x 4 =** **11 x 4 =** **12 x 4 =**

7 x 4 = 3 x 4 = 9 x 4 =

6 x 4 = 11 x 4 = 8 x 4 =

4 x 4 = 5 x 4 = 12 x 4 =

2 x 4 = 10 x 4 = 1 x 4 =

2 x 5 =

6 x 4 =

9 x 6 =

8 x 3 =

10 x 11 =

12 x 3 =

6 x 8 =

5 x 7 =

3 x 9 =

6 x 12 =

4 x 9 =

7 x 6 =

9 x 9 =

8 x 5 =

4 x 4 =

5 x 5 =

6 x 6 =

3 x 3 =

10 x 10 =

2 x 2 =

Review of 4

Try hard now to get them all right!

If you get some wrong, write them out a few times until you know them and then get your parent or teacher to retest you.

3	7	4	9	10	6
x 4	x 4	x 4	x 4	x 4	x 4
___	___	___	___	___	___

5	12	2	8	1	11
x 4	x 4	x 4	x 4	x 4	x 4
___	___	___	___	___	___

4 x 4 = ...	4 x 6 = ...	4 x 9 = ...	4 x 11 = ...
4 x 7 = ...	4 x 11 = ...	4 x 5 = ...	4 x 12 = ...
4 x 3 = ...	4 x 1 = ...	4 x 8 = ...	4 x 2 = ...

1	10	7	3	5	12
x 4	x 4	x 4	x 4	x 4	x 4
___	___	___	___	___	___

4	8	6	11	2	9
x 4	x 4	x 4	x 4	x 4	x 4
___	___	___	___	___	___

The Eight Times Multiplication Table

1 x 8 = 8	7 x 8 = 56
2 x 8 = 16	8 x 8 = 64
3 x 8 = 24	9 x 8 = 72
4 x 8 = 32	10x 8 = 80
5 x 8 = 40	11x 8 = 88
6 x 8 = 48	12x 8 = 96

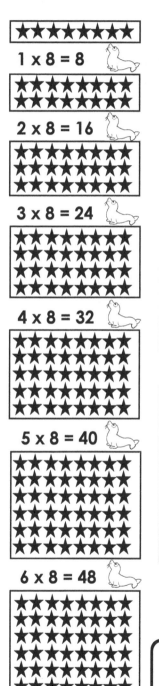

1 x 8 = 8

2 x 8 = 16

3 x 8 = 24

4 x 8 = 32

5 x 8 = 40

6 x 8 = 48

7 x 8 = 56

8 x 8 = 64

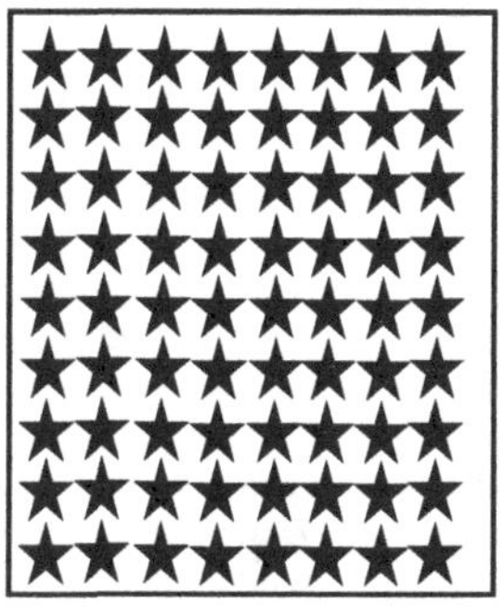

9 x 8 = 72

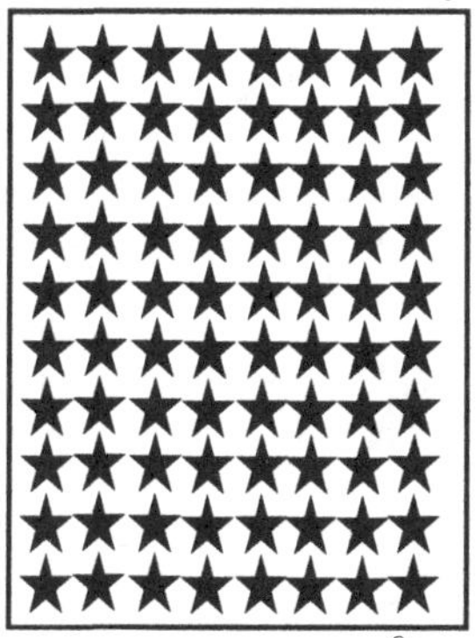

10 x 8 = 80

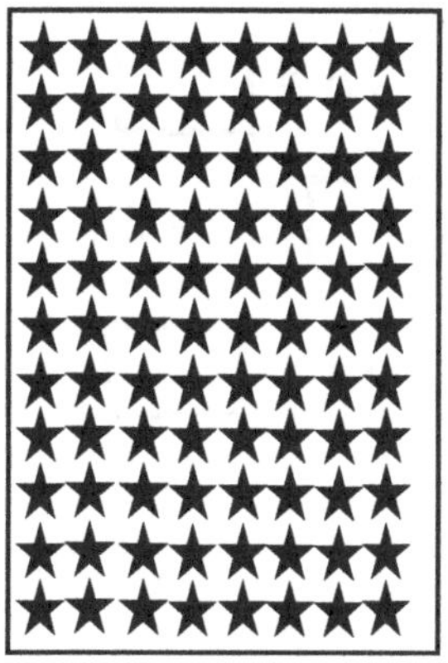

11 x 8 = 88

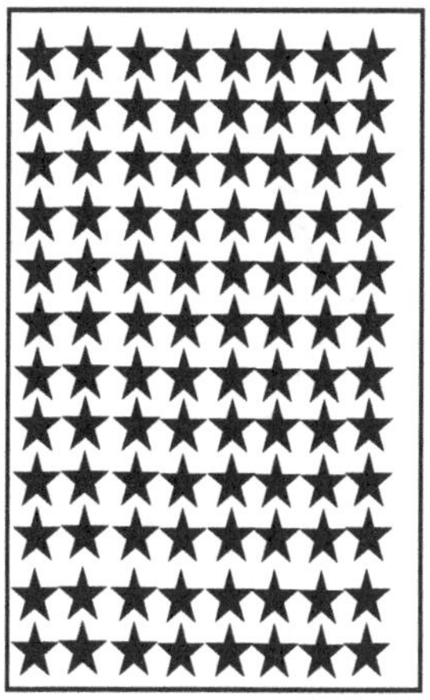

12 x 8 = 96

You only have **4 new tables** to learn in the 8 Times Tables!

Colour in the small seals next to the tables that you know.

Practise the new tables in the big seals above.

Multiplication by 8

Write out the eight times multiplication table twice.

Complete the 8 Times Tables:

1 x 8 = ☐   ☐ x 8 = 16   3 x 8 = ☐

☐ x 8 = 32   5 x 8 = ☐   ☐ x 8 = 48

7 x 8 = ☐   ☐ x 8 = 64   9 x 8 = ☐

☐ x 8 = 80   11 x 8 = ☐   ☐ x 8 = 96

1 x 8 = 8	**7 x 8 = 56**
2 x 8 = 16	**8 x 8 = 64**
3 x 8 = 24	**9 x 8 = 72**
4 x 8 = 32	**10x 8 = 80**
5 x 8 = 40	**11x 8 = 88**
6 x 8 = 48	**12x 8 = 96**

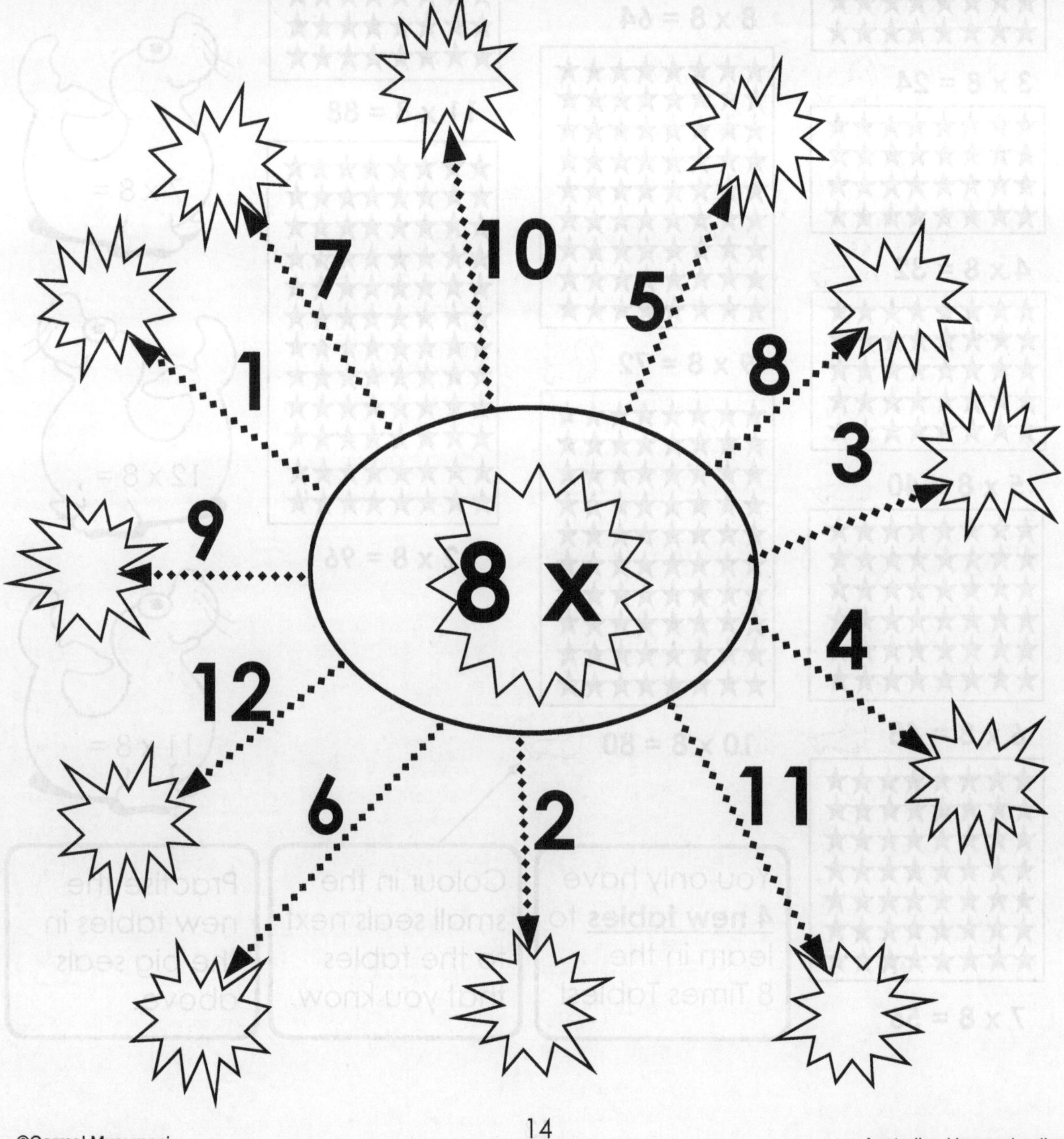

Multiplication by 8

Write out the eight times multiplication table twice.

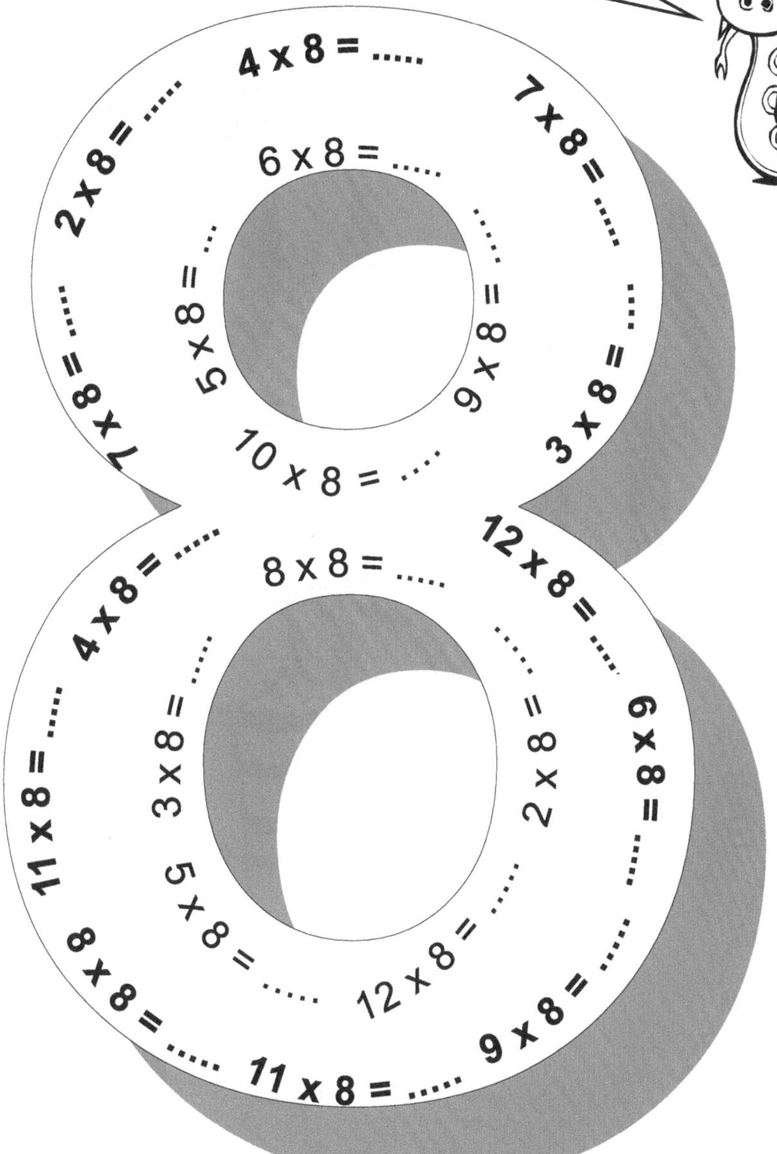

2	3	4	5	6
x 5	x 6	x 4	x 9	x 5

7	8	9	10	11
x 5	x 6	x 4	x 9	x 5

12 x 5 =___ 2 x 6 =___ 3 x 4 =___ 4 x 9 =___

Multiplication by 8

Write out the eight times multiplication table twice.

Can you find and answer the 8 times tables on the zebra?

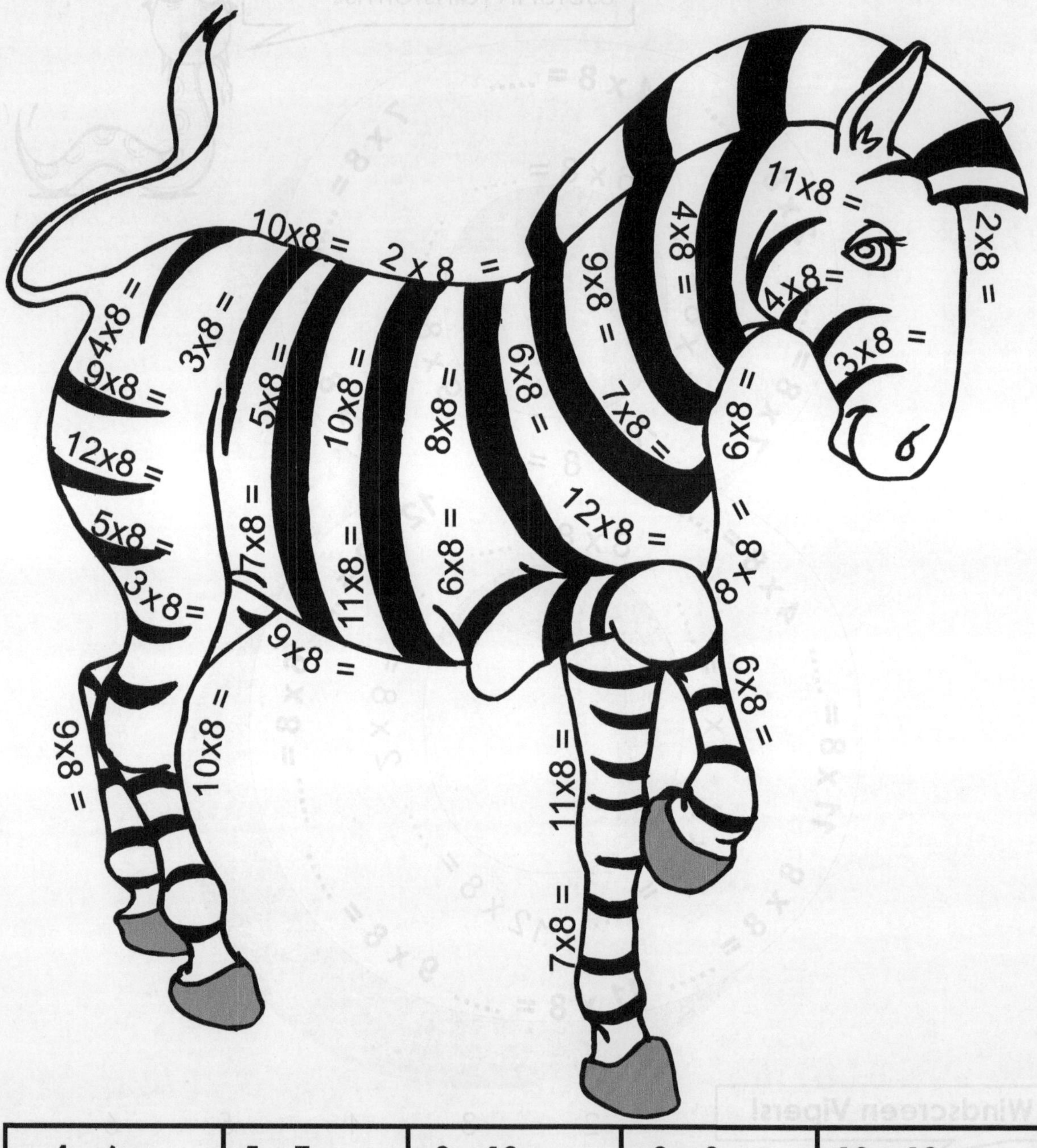

4 x 6 = ___	**5 x 7 =** ___	**2 x 12 =** ___	**8 x 3 =** ___	**10 x 10 =** ___
6 x 9 = ___	**3 x 11 =** ___	**4 x 4 =** ___	**12 x 4 =** ___	**7 x 4 =** ___
3 x 5 = ___	**12 x 5 =** ___	**10 x 11 =** ___	**4 x 8 =** ___	**6 x 5 =** ___
2 x 9 = ___	**7 x 6 =** ___	**5 x 9 =** ___	**9 x 4 =** ___	**12 x 6 =** ___

Multiplication by 8

Write out the eight times multiplication table twice.

What do owls eat for breakfast?

Starting at the star, follow the direction of the arrow and complete the tables.

★ 6   10   9   4   7   3
x 8   x 8   x 8 x 8 x 8 x 8

11   1   8   2   12   5
x 8   x 8 x 8 x 8 x 8   x 8

8 x 4 = ...   8 x 6 = ...   8 x 9 = ...   8 x 11 = ...

8 x 7 = ...   8 x 11 = ...   8 x 5 = ...   8 x 12 = ...

8 x 3 = ...   8 x 1 = ...   8 x 8 = ...   8 x 2 = ...

Keep writing out your tables twice every day.
This will help you to remember them!

Hoot Loops!

10 x 3 = ...   10 x 5 = ...
10 x 4 = ...   10 x 6 = ...
10 x 2 = ...
10 x 8 = ...
10x10 = ...
10x11 = ...
10x12 = ...

9 x 2 = ...   9 x 5 = ...
9 x 4 = ...   9 x 3 = ...
9 x 6 = ...

9x10 = ...
9x12 = ...
9 x 9 = ...
9x11 = ...
9 x 8 = ...

©Carmel Musumeci
Coroneos Publications

Australian Homeschooling

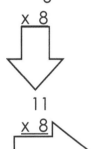

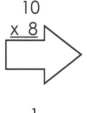

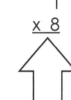

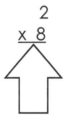

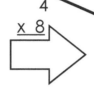

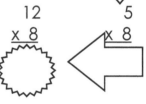

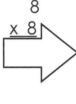

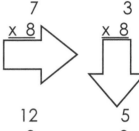

Multiplication by 8

Write out the eight times multiplication table twice.

1 x 8 =

5 x 8 =

10 x 8 =

7 x 8 =

6 x 8 =

9 x 8 =

5 x 8 =

2 x 8 =

1 x 8 =

8 x 8 =

12 x 8 =

4 x 8 =

8 x 8 =

11 x 8 =

6 x 8 =

4 x 8 =

3 x 8 =

12 x 8 =

9 x 8 =

10 x 8 =

2 x 8 =

11 x 8 =

3 x 8 =

7 x 8 =

6 x .... = 6	6 x .... = 60	6 x .... = 24
6 x .... = 18	6 x .... = 48	6 x .... = 30
6 x .... = 36	6 x .... = 42	6 x .... = 54
6 x .... = 66	6 x .... = 72	6 x .... = 42
6 x .... = 54	6 x .... = 12	6 x .... = 18

Multiplication by 8

Write out the eight times multiplication table twice.

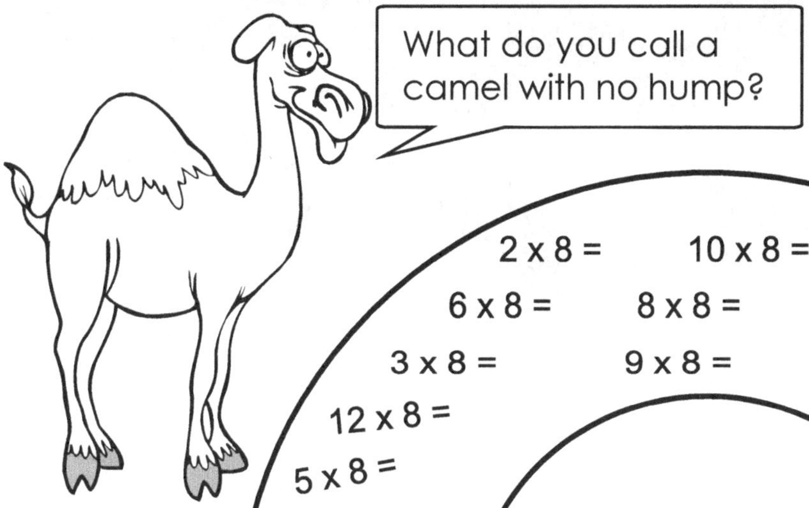
What do you call a camel with no hump?

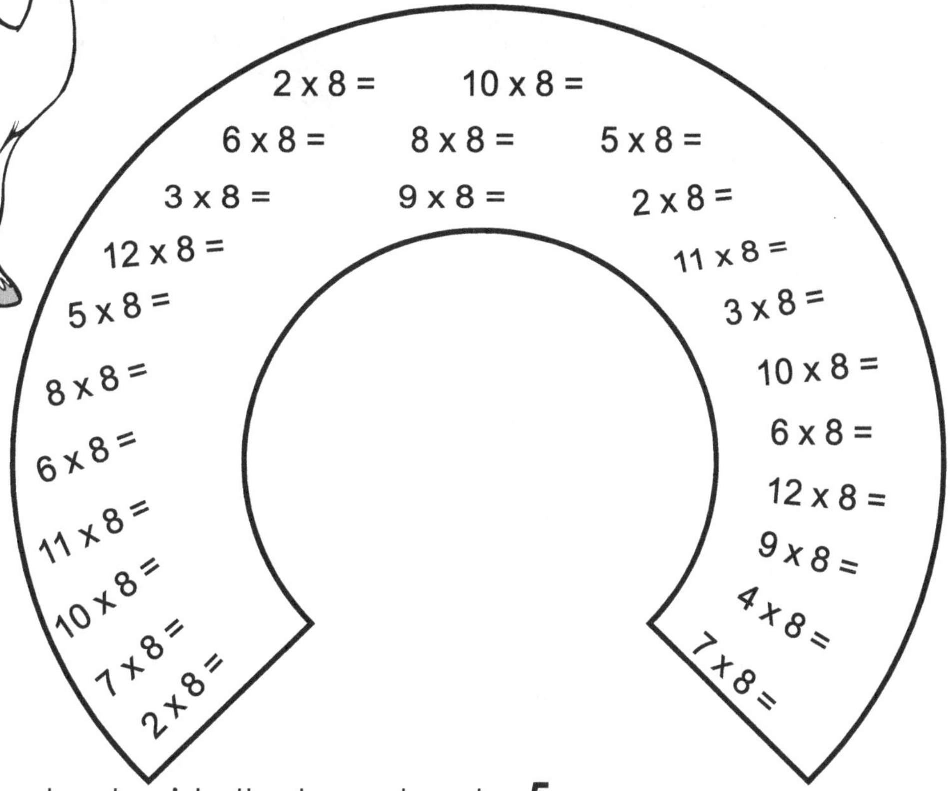
2 x 8 =
10 x 8 =
6 x 8 =
8 x 8 =
5 x 8 =
3 x 8 =
9 x 8 =
2 x 8 =
12 x 8 =
11 x 8 =
5 x 8 =
3 x 8 =
8 x 8 =
10 x 8 =
6 x 8 =
6 x 8 =
12 x 8 =
11 x 8 =
9 x 8 =
10 x 8 =
4 x 8 =
7 x 8 =
7 x 8 =
2 x 8 =

Multiply the number beside the horseshoe by **5**.
Write the product inside it.

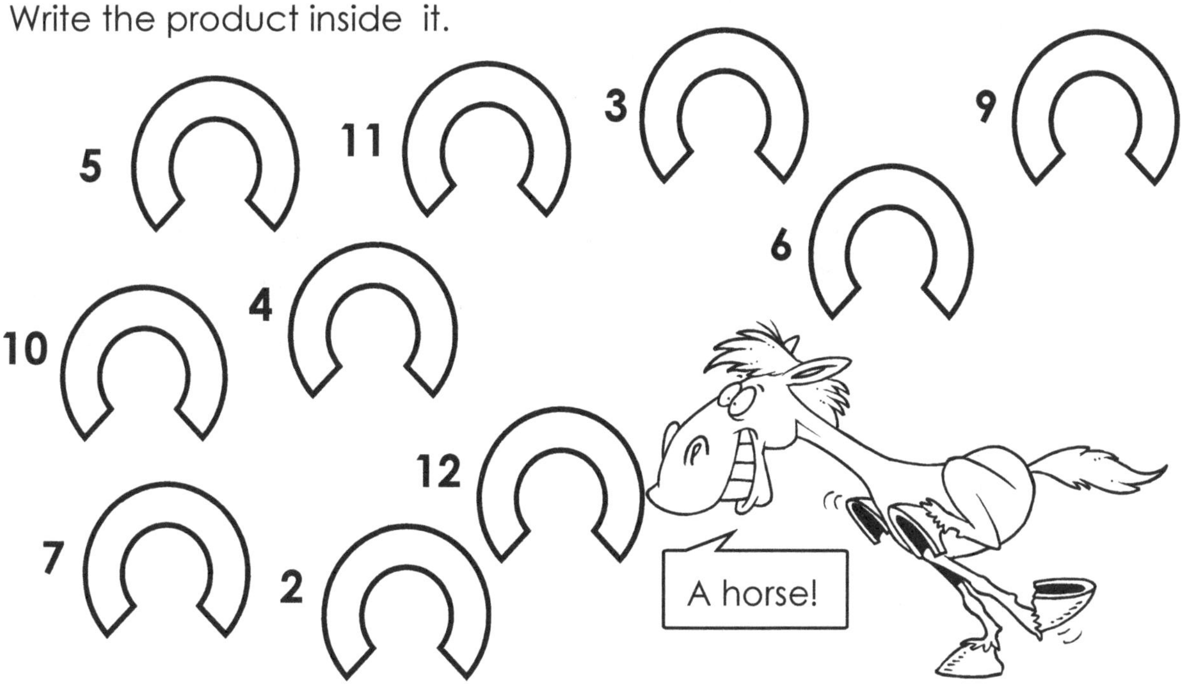
5
11
3
9
6
10
4
12
7
2
A horse!

Multiplication by 8

Write out the eight times multiplication table twice.

$$\begin{array}{c} 10 \\ \times\ 8 \\\hline \end{array}$$

$$\begin{array}{c} 4 \\ \times\ 8 \\\hline \end{array}$$

$$\begin{array}{c} 5 \\ \times\ 8 \\\hline \end{array}$$

$$\begin{array}{c} 2 \\ \times\ 8 \\\hline \end{array}$$

$$\begin{array}{c} 11 \\ \times\ 8 \\\hline \end{array}$$

$$\begin{array}{c} 12 \\ \times\ 8 \\\hline \end{array}$$

$$\begin{array}{c} 9 \\ \times\ 8 \\\hline \end{array}$$

$$\begin{array}{c} 8 \\ \times\ 8 \\\hline \end{array}$$

$$\begin{array}{c} 6 \\ \times\ 8 \\\hline \end{array}$$

$$\begin{array}{c} 4 \\ \times\ 8 \\\hline \end{array}$$

$$\begin{array}{c} 12 \\ \times\ 8 \\\hline \end{array}$$

$$\begin{array}{c} 3 \\ \times\ 8 \\\hline \end{array}$$

$$\begin{array}{c} 7 \\ \times\ 8 \\\hline \end{array}$$

$$\begin{array}{c} 4 \\ \times\ 8 \\\hline \end{array}$$

$$\begin{array}{c} 8 \\ \times\ 8 \\\hline \end{array}$$

$$\begin{array}{c} 5 \\ \times\ 8 \\\hline \end{array}$$

$$\begin{array}{c} 10 \\ \times\ 8 \\\hline \end{array}$$

$$\begin{array}{c} 11 \\ \times\ 8 \\\hline \end{array}$$

$$\begin{array}{c} 6 \\ \times\ 8 \\\hline \end{array}$$

$$\begin{array}{c} 9 \\ \times\ 8 \\\hline \end{array}$$

$$\begin{array}{c} 7 \\ \times\ 8 \\\hline \end{array}$$

3 x 5 =	3 x 7 =	3 x 11 =	3 x 4 =	3 x 8 =
3 x 6 =	3 x 12 =	3 x 10 =	3 x 2 =	3 x 9 =
3 x 3 =	3 x 8 =	3 x 6 =	3 x 7 =	3 x 11 =
3 x 9 =	3 x 10 =	3 x 5 =	3 x 12 =	3 x 3 =
3 x 4 =	3 x 2 =	3 x 6 =	3 x 8 =	3 x 5 =

20

Australian Homeschooling

Multiplication by 8

Write out the eight times multiplication table twice.

6x8 =
9x8 =
8x8 =
7x8 =

3 x 8 =	11 x 8 =	6 x 8 =
10 x 8 =	7 x 8 =	4 x 8 =
12 x 8 =	5 x 8 =	9 x 8 =
8 x 8 =	1 x 8 =	2 x 8 =

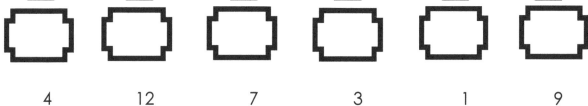

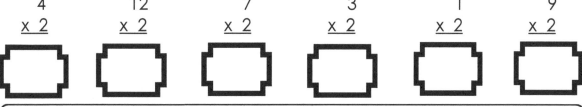

11x8=
4x8 =
10x8=
3x8 =
What's big, white, furry and found in out-back Australia?
5x8 =
12x8=
A VERY lost Polar Bear!

2	5	10	8	11	6
x 2	x 2	x 2	x 2	x 2	x 2

4	12	7	3	1	9
x 2	x 2	x 2	x 2	x 2	x 2

2 x 5 =	2 x 8 =	2 x 10 =	2 x 9 =	2 x 11 =
2 x 3 =	2 x 7 =	2 x 1 =	2 x 12 =	2 x 2 =
6 x 7 =	11 x 10 =	5 x 5 =	8 x 6 =	12 x 4 =

Review of 8

Jumpin'- Jackaroos,
It's time for another review!

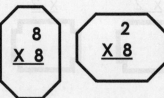

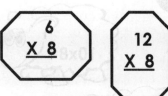

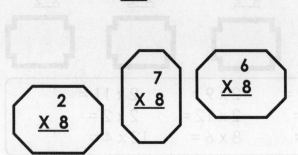

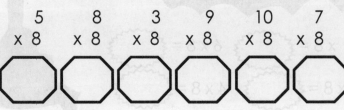

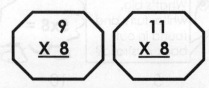

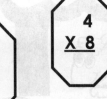

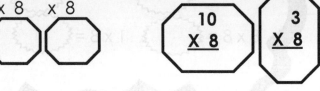

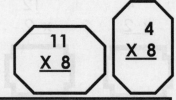

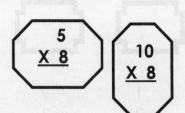

Remember to colour them in on page 4,
If you get them all correct!

5   8   3   9   10   7
x 8   x 8   x 8   x 8   x 8   x 8

11   4   5   12   2   1
x 8   x 8   x 8   x 8   x 8   x 8

10   3
X 8   X 8

6   12
X 8   X 8

4
X 8

8
X 8

5   7
X 8   X 8

3   9   12   9   11
X 8   X 8   X 8   X 8   X 8

5   10
X 8   X 8

1   8   2
X 8   X 8   X 8

2   7   6
X 8   X 8   X 8

11   4
X 8   X 8

After you get all of these right,
you only have another
6 new Tables to learn!

22

©Carmel Musumeci
Coroneos Publications

Australian Homeschooling

The Twelve Times Multiplication Table

1 x 12 = 12	7 x 12 = 84
2 x 12 = 24	8 x 12 = 96
3 x 12 = 36	9 x 12 = 108
4 x 12 = 48	10x 12 = 120
5 x 12 = 60	11x 12 = 132
6 x 12 = 72	12x 12 = 144

Write out the twelve times multiplication table twice.

You have learnt all of the 12 Times Tables in the other Tables, except for **two**!

They are: **11 x 12 = 132**
12 x 12 = 144

1 x 12 =	3 x 12 =
2 x 12 =	9 x 12 =
3 x 12 =	2 x 12 =
4 x 12 =	10 x 12 =
5 x 12 =	4 x 12 =
6 x 12 =	8 x 12 =
7 x 12 =	11 x 12 =
8 x 12 =	5 x 12 =
9 x 12 =	12 x 12 =
10 x 12 =	1 x 12 =
11 x 12 =	7 x 12 =
12 x 12 =	6 x 12 =

11 x 12 = 132

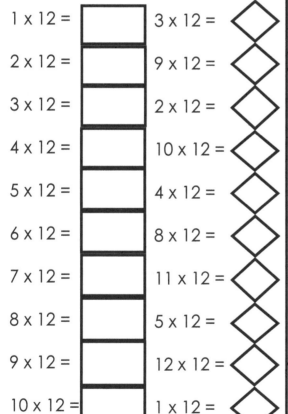

12 x 12 = 144

Gross Tables! (12 x 12 = 144 or gross)
To play this game you'll need an egg carton with numbers 1 to 12 written on the bottom and 2 buttons. Close the lid and shake the carton. Give the answer to the two numbers multiplied - this is 1 point. Keep score and see who wins!

Multiplication by 12

Write out the twelve times multiplication table twice.

What should you do if you see a gorilla sitting at your school desk?

3 x 12 =	**l**	8 x12 =	**r**
4 x 12 =	**h**	9 x12 =	**w**
5 x 12 =	**e**	10x12 =	**m**
6 x 12 =	**o**	11x12 =	**t**
7 x 12 =	**i**	12x12 =	**s**

Work out the answer by filling in the blanks below.

___ ___ ___
144 84 132

___ ___ ___ ___ ___ ___ ___ ___ ___
144 72 120 60 108 48 60 96 60

___ ___ ___ ___ !
60 36 144 60

Multiply the factors and write the product inside the orange.

5 x 12 = 

7 x 12 = 

11 x 12 = 

4 x 12 = 

10 x 12 = 

6 x 12 = 

8 x 12 = 

3 x 12 = 

12 x 12 = 

9 x 12 = 

2 x 12 = 

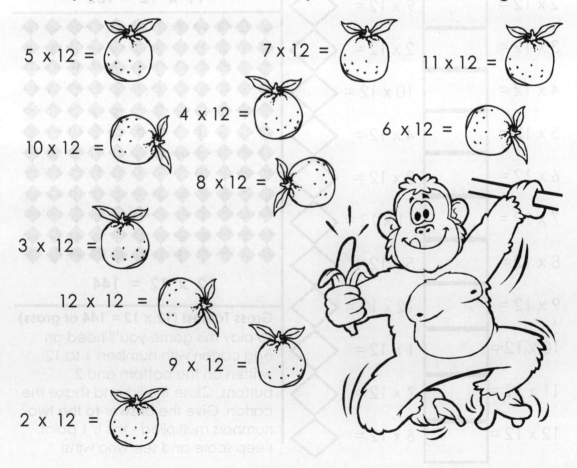

Multiplication by 12

Write out the twelve times multiplication table twice.

12 x 3 =

12 x 7 =

12 x 6 =

12 x 4 =

12 x 10 =

12 x 2 =

12 x 11 =

12 x 8 =

12 x 9 =

12 x 12 =

12 x 5 =

12 x 12 =

12 x11 =

12 x 7 =

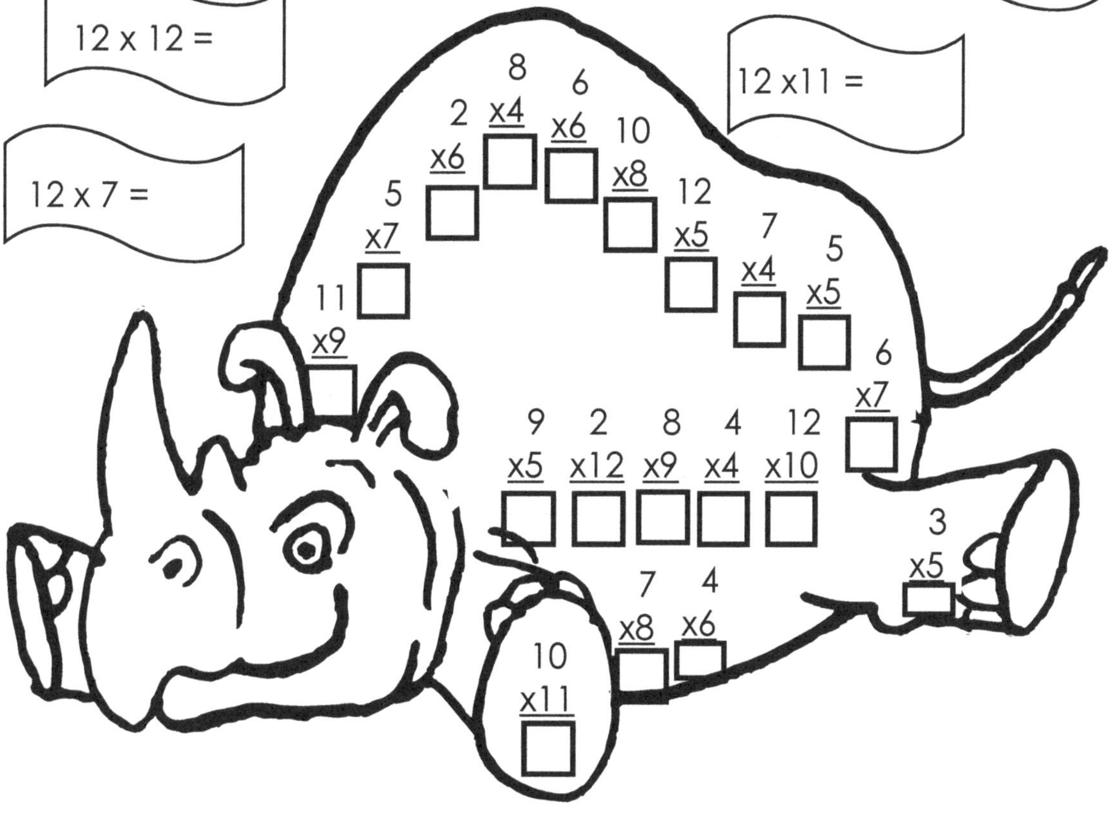

Multiplication by 12

Write out the twelve times multiplication table twice.

What happened to the duck who flew upside down? **He quacked up!**

4 x 12 =

12 x 12 =

9 x 12 =

10 x 12 =

8 x 12 =

3 x 12 =

5 x 12 =

11 x 12 =

4 x 12 =

7 x 12 =

6 x 12 =

8 x 12 =

10 x 12 =

12 x 12 =

9 x 12 =

11 x 12 =

7 x 12 =

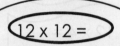

4 x 4	6 x 4	9 x 4	10 x 4	2 x 4	5 x 4
11 x 4	1 x 4	7 x 4	3 x 4	12 x 4	8 x 4

Write out the twelve times multiplication table twice.

12	11	10	9	8	7
x 12	x 12	x 12	x 12	x 12	x 12

6	5	4	3	2	1
x 12	x 12	x 12	x 12	x 12	x 12

10	12			11	9
x 12	x 12			x 12	x 12

12	12	12	12	12	12
x 3	x 8	x 5	x 12	x 7	x 2

12	12	12	12	12	12
x 4	x 10	x 1	x 9	x 6	x 11

9 x 2 = ...   7 x 5 = ...   6 x 7 = ...   9 x 6 = ...

3 x 4 = ...   5 x 12 = ...   10 x 10 = ...   11 x 9 = ...   10 x 8 = ...

12 x 6 = ...   7 x 8 = ...   4 x 8 = ...   7 x 9 = ...   8 x 8 = ...   7 x 7 = ...

9 x 4 = ...   6 x 5 = ...   10 x 11 = ...   6 x 7 = ...   9 x 9 = ...

12 x 3 = ...   4 x 7 = ...

©Carmel Musumeci
Coroneos Publications

Australian Homeschooling

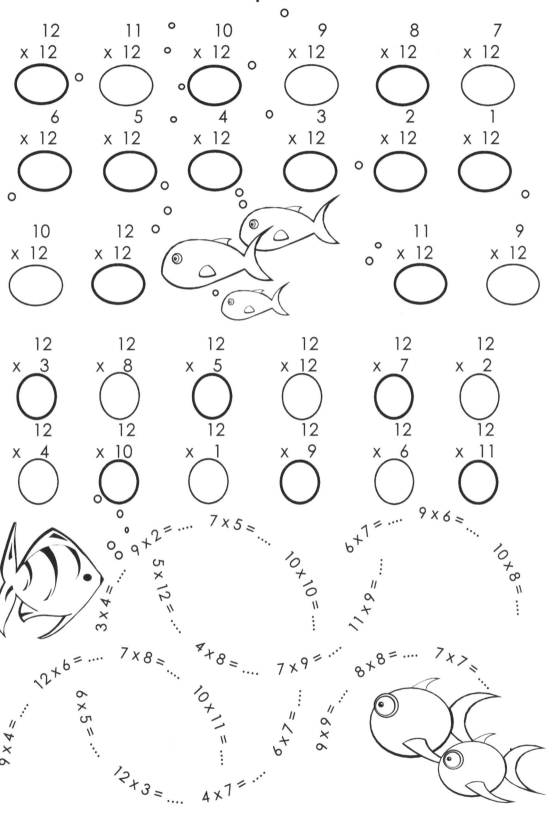

Multiplication by 12

Write out the twelve times multiplication table twice.

___ x 12 = 96   ___ x 12 = 36   ___ x 12 = 144
___ x 12 = 108   ___ x 12 = 120   ___ x 12 = 12
___ x 12 = 60   ___ x 12 = 72   ___ x 12 = 84
___ x 12 = 24   ___ x 12 = 132   ___ x 12 = 48

So how do fleas travel?

4 x 12 =   11 x 12 =   5 x 12 =

10 x 12 =

8 x 12 =   9 x 12 =   3 x 12 =   6 x 12 =

7 x 12 =   12 x 12 =   9 x 12 =   12 x 12 =

| 8 | 5 | 7 | 11 | 2 | 6 | 9 | 3 |
| x 4 | x 6 | x 5 | x 2 | x 10 | x 4 | x 6 | x 8 |

| 4 | 8 | 4 | 12 |
| x 4 | x 6 | x 5 | x 2 |

| 9 | 12 | 9 | 8 |
| x 4 | x 6 | x 5 | x 2 |

| 5 | 7 | 8 | 7 |
| x 4 | x 6 | x 5 | x 2 |

They itch-hike!

28

Australian Homeschooling

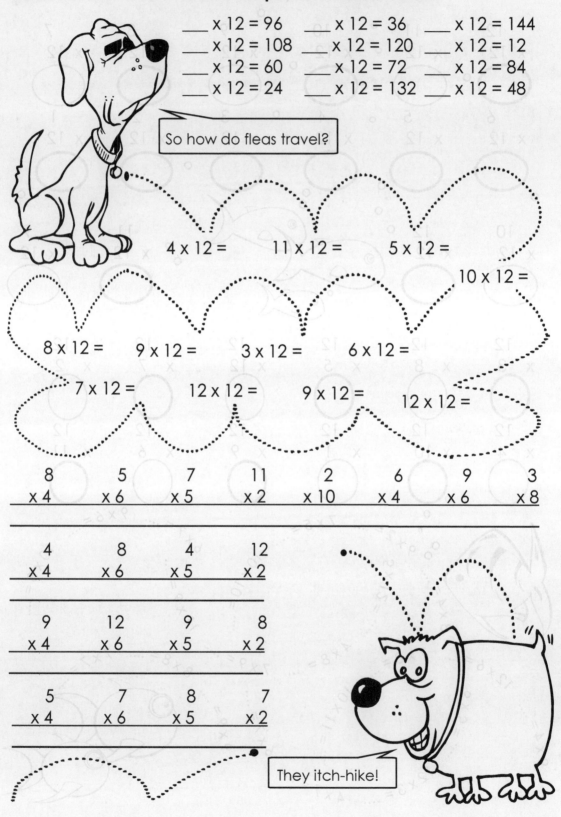

Multiplication by 12

Write out the twelve times multiplication table twice.

Which set of tables can you finish the fastest, the hare's or the tortoise's? Time yourself and see who wins the race!

2 x 8 =

4 x 12 =

11 x 12 =

9 x 8 =

1 x 12 =

3 x 12 =

7 x 12 =   12 x 12 =   5 x 8 =

6 x 12 =

7 x 8 =

5 x 12 =

11 x 12 =

8 x 12 =

10 x 12 =

9 x 8 =

Hare's Time:_____   Tortoise's Time:_____

6 x 8 =

5 x 12 =

1 x 8 =

12 x 8 =

3 x 8 =

4 x 8 =

7 x 12 =   6 x 12 =   5 x 8 =

2 x 12 =

9 x 12 =

7 x 12 =

12 x 12 =

10 x 8 =

8 x 8 =

11 x 8 =

©Carmel Musumeci
Coroneos Publications

Australian Homeschooling

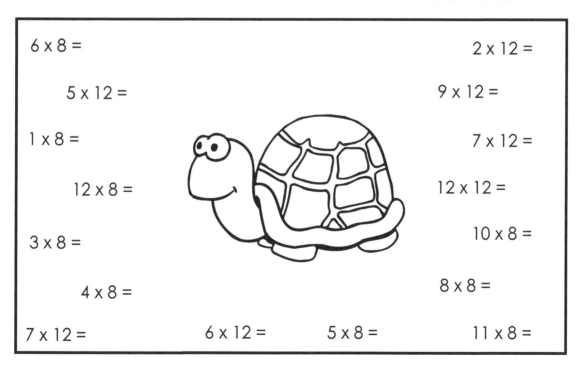

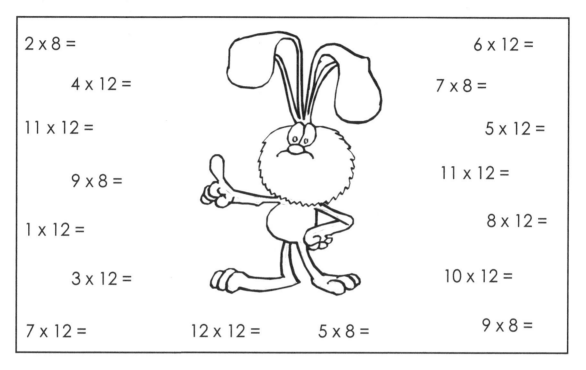

Multiplication by 12

Write out the twelve times multiplication table twice.

©Carmel Musumeci
Coroneos Publications

Australian Homeschooling

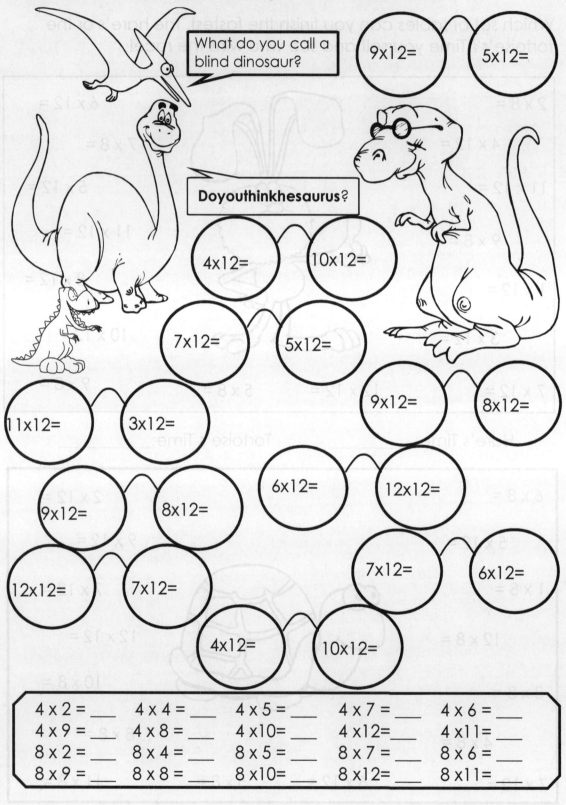

Multiplication by 12

Write out the twelve times multiplication table twice.

5
x 12

3
x 12

8
x 12

10
x 12

2
x 12

7
x 12

6
x 12

9
x 12

12
x 12

4
x 12

11
x 12

8
x 12

7
x 12

12
x 12

9
x 12

6
x 12

4
x 12

Fill in the missing factors:

4 x ☐ = 24   6 x ☐ = 48   7 x ☐ = 28   5 x ☐ = 35

3 x ☐ = 36   8 x ☐ = 80   11 x ☐ = 55   9 x ☐ = 54

2 x ☐ = 22   6 x ☐ = 72   8 x ☐ = 72   3 x ☐ = 21

31

©Carmel Musumeci
Coroneos Publications

Australian Homeschooling

Review of 12

Wallaby-playing-a-Kazoo,
It's time for your Review!

3 x 12 = ⬠   12 x 12 = ⬠

6 x 12 = ⬠   10 x 12 = ⬠

4 x 12 = ⬠   5 x 12 = ⬠

8 x 12 = ⬠   7 x 12 = ⬠   6 x 12 = ⬠   9 x 12 = ⬠

11 x 12 = ⬠   2 x 12 = ⬠   12 x 12 = ⬠   6 x 12 = ⬠

1 x 12 = ⬠   9 x 12 = ⬠   11 x 12 = ⬠   8 x 12 = ⬠

12x8 =
4 x 4 =
5 x 9 =

6 x 5 =
5 x 3 =
4 x 7 =

6 x 6 =
4 x 9 =
3 x 7 =

5 x 8 =
2x11 =
10x6 =

7 x 8 =
9 x 9 =
11x6 =

3 x 3 =
11x5 =
5 x 9 =

2 x10=
3 x 6 =
4 x 3 =

8 x 4 =
3 x 9 =
7 x 6 =

12 x6=
5 x 5 =
9 x 4 =

10x10=
7 x 6 =
2 x 2 =

4 x 2 =
11x10=
3 x 8 =

7 x 5 =
8 x11=
6 x10=

8 x 8 =
6 x 9 =
4 x 5 =

12x9 =
6 x 8 =
5x12 =

2 x 3 =
9 x11 =
10x5 =

32

©Carmel Musumeci
Coroneos Publications

Australian Homeschooling

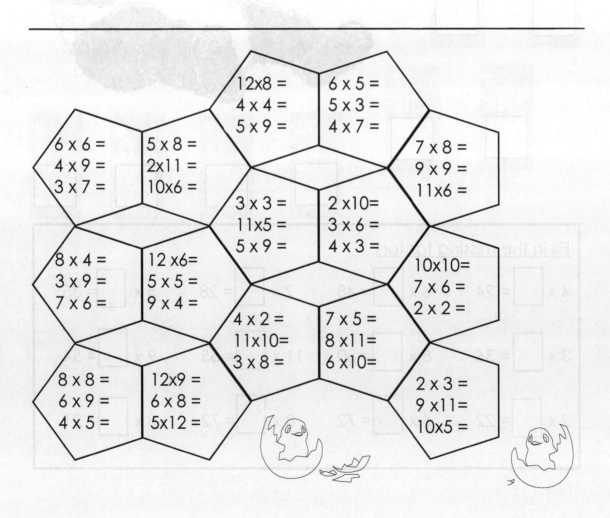

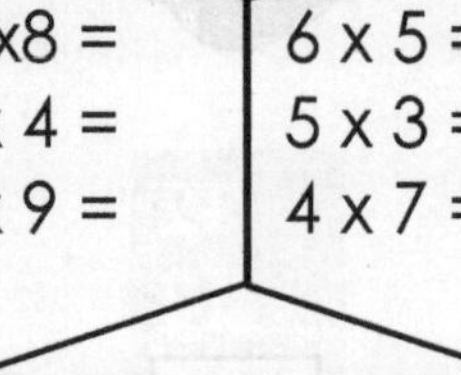

The Seven Times Multiplication Table

1 x 7 = 7	7 x 7 = 49
2 x 7 = 14	8 x 7 = 56
3 x 7 = 21	9 x 7 = 63
4 x 7 = 28	10x 7 = 70
5 x 7 = 35	11x 7 = 77
6 x 7 = 42	12x 7 = 84

Write out the seven times multiplication table twice.

There are only **2 new tables** for you to learn! The ants show you the ones you know.

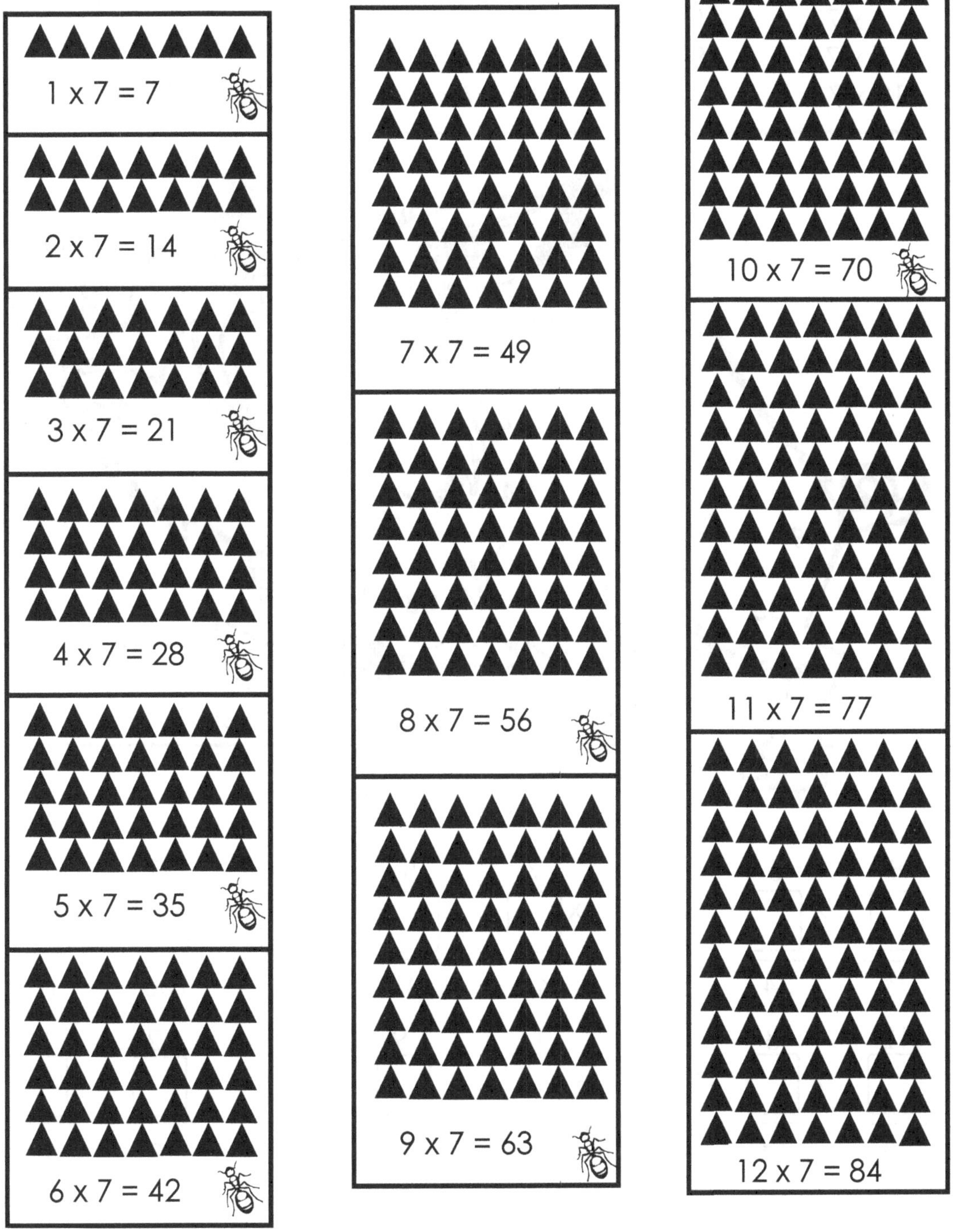

Multiplication by 7

Write out the seven times multiplication table twice.

On the hog below are the answers for the tables in the box.
Cross them out as you use them.

1 x 7 =	2 x 7 =	3 x 7 =
4 x 7 =	5 x 7 =	6 x 7 =
7 x 7 =	8 x 7 =	9 x 7 =
10 x 7 =	11 x 7 =	12 x 7 =

Why don't pigs learn how to drive?

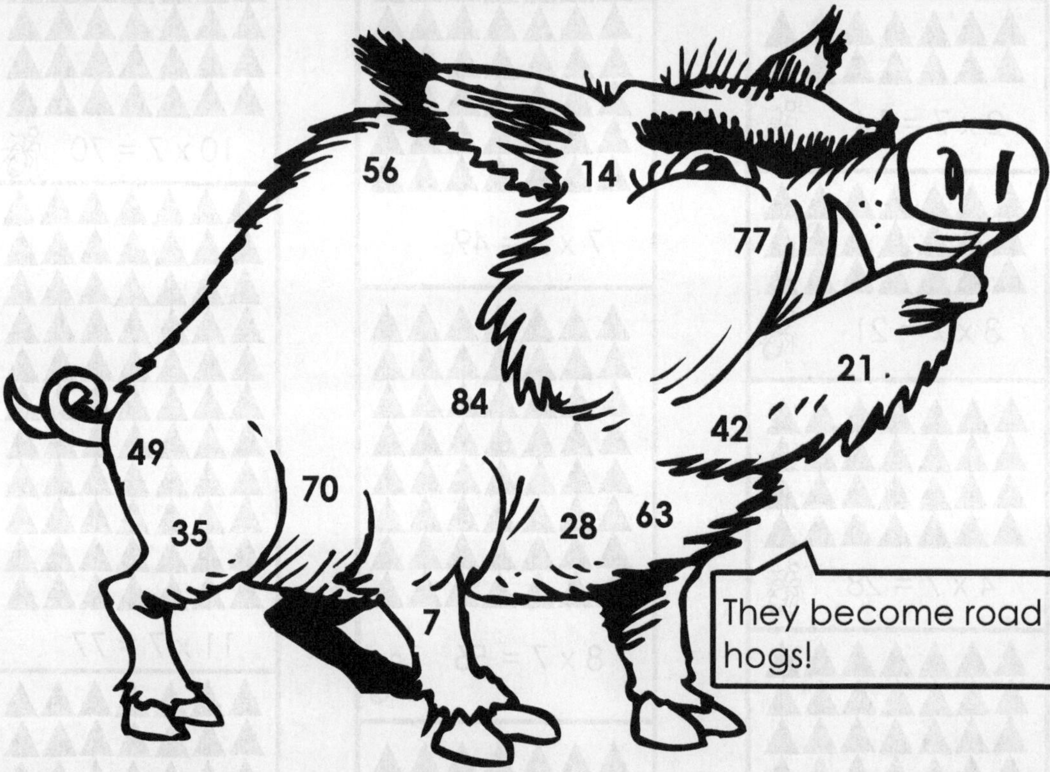

They become road hogs!

8	6	3	7	5	9	10	4
x ☐	x ☐	x ☐	x ☐	x ☐	x ☐	x ☐	x ☐
24	24	21	42	45	54	100	16
12	8	2	11	9	6	12	3
x ☐	x ☐	x ☐	x ☐	x ☐	x ☐	x ☐	x ☐
96	64	14	132	81	48	48	27

Multiplication by 7

Write out the seven times multiplication table twice.

2	6	9	10	4
x 7	x 7	x 7	x 7	x 7
7	1	11	3	12
x 7	x 7	x 7	x 7	x 7
3	8	5	12	10
x 7	x 7	x 7	x 7	x 7
6	7	4	9	12
x 7	x 7	x 7	x 7	x 7

___ x 7 = 35 ___ x 7 = 84 ___ x 7 = 49 ___ x 7 = 77

___ x 7 = 7 ___ x 7 = 21 ___ x 7 = 70 ___ x 7 = 56

___ x 7 = 28 ___ x 7 = 14 ___ x 7 = 63 ___ x 7 = 42

How fast can you finish these?

4 x 8 = ___	3 x 9 = ___	12 x 5 = ___	9 x 8 = ___
7 x 6 = ___	10 x 11 = ___	6 x 4 = ___	5 x 7 = ___
9 x 6 = ___	8 x 12 = ___	7 x 8 = ___	6 x 5 = ___
12 x 9 = ___	3 x 11 = ___	4 x 12 = ___	8 x 8 = ___

Multiplication by 7

Write out the seven times multiplication table twice.

2 x 7 = _ _ _ _

6 x 7 = _ _ _ _

11 x 7 = _ _ _ _

4 x 7 = _ _ _ _

9 x 7 = _ _ _ _

3 x 7 = _ _ _ _

10 x 7 = _ _ _ _

5 x 7 = _ _ _ _

7 x 7 = _ _ _ _

1 x 7 = _ _ _ _

12 x 7 = _ _ _ _

4 x 7 = _ _ _ _

8 x 7 = _ _ _ _

5 x 7 = _ _ _ _

11 x 7 = _ _ _ _

9 x 7 = _ _ _ _

7 x 7 = ...

7 x 3 = ...

7 x 4 = ...

7 x 8 = ...

7 x 9 = ...

7 x 11 = ...

7 x 2 = ...

7 x 12 = ...

7 x 10 = ...

7 x 5 = ...

7 x 6 = ...

7 x 12 = ...

7 x 7 = ...

7	8
x	x
5	8

6	3
x	x
12	9

10	4
x	x
11	9

7	12
x	x
6	8

9	6
x	x
9	8

Australian Homeschooling

Multiplication by 7

Write out the seven times multiplication table twice.

4 x 7 =

7 x 7 =

11 x 7 =

8 x 7 =

2 x 7 =

3 x 7 =

6 x 7 =

8 x 7 =

11 x 7 =

4 x 7 =

7 x 7 =

9 x 7 =

5 x 7 =

9 x 7 =

12 x 7 =

10 x 7 =

6 x 7 =

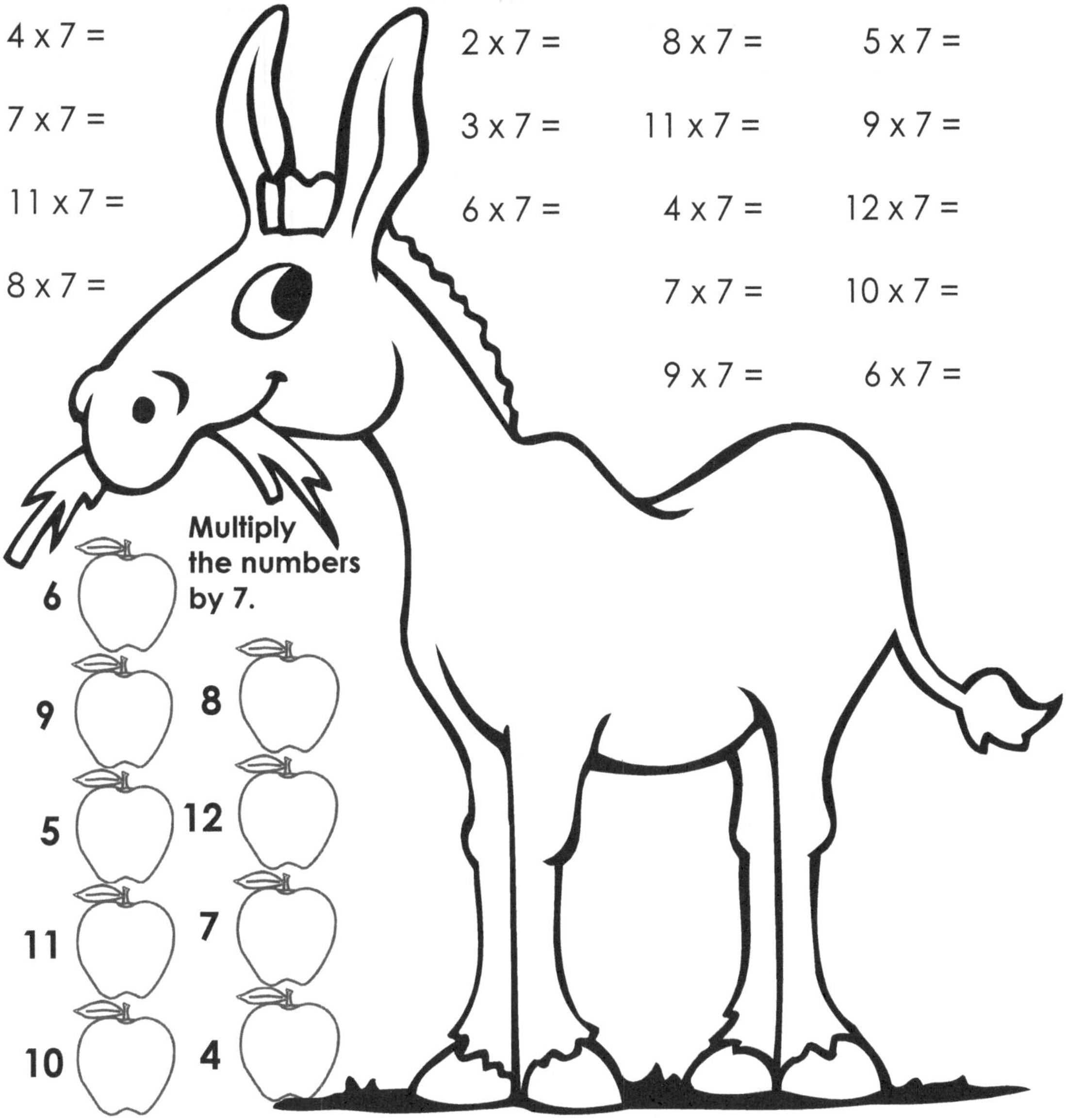

Multiply the numbers by 7.

6

9

5

11

10

8

12

7

4

What do you call a three legged donkey?

A wonkey?!

| 5 X 6 | 4 X 8 | 9 X 7 | 7 X 4 |

| 8 X 6 | 4 X12 | 6 X 6 | 2 X 9 | | 5 X 9 | | 12 X11 | 3 X 4 | 10 X 9 | 11 X10 |

37

Australian Homeschooling

Multiplication by 7

Write out the seven times multiplication table twice.

5 x 7 =........	
4 x 7 =........	
8 x 7 =........	
3 x 7 =........	
9 x 7 =........	
2 x 7 =........	
7 x 7 =........	
6 x 7 =........	

12 x 7 =.....–..
6 x 7 =.....–..
11 x 7 =.....–..
5 x 7 =.....–..
1 x 7 =.....–..
10 x 7 =.....–..
8 x 7 =.....–..
7 x 7 =.....–..

7 x 2 = _ _ _
7 x 5 = _ _ _
7 x 11 = _ _ _
7 x 10 = _ _ _
7 x 4 = _ _ _
7 x 9 = _ _ _
7 x 7 = _ _ _
7 x 6 = _ _ _
7 x 3 = _ _ _

.... x 7 = 21
.... x 7 = 77
.... x 7 = 35
.... x 7 = 84
.... x 7 = 63
.... x 7 = 28
.... x 7 = 56
.... x 7 = 49

8 x 7 = _ _ _ _

7 x 7 = _ _ _ _

12 x 7 = _ _ _ _

9 x 7 = _ _ _ _

6 x 7	4 x 7	3 x 7	5 x 7
☐	☐	☐	☐

What game do cows play at parties?

Moo-sical Chairs!

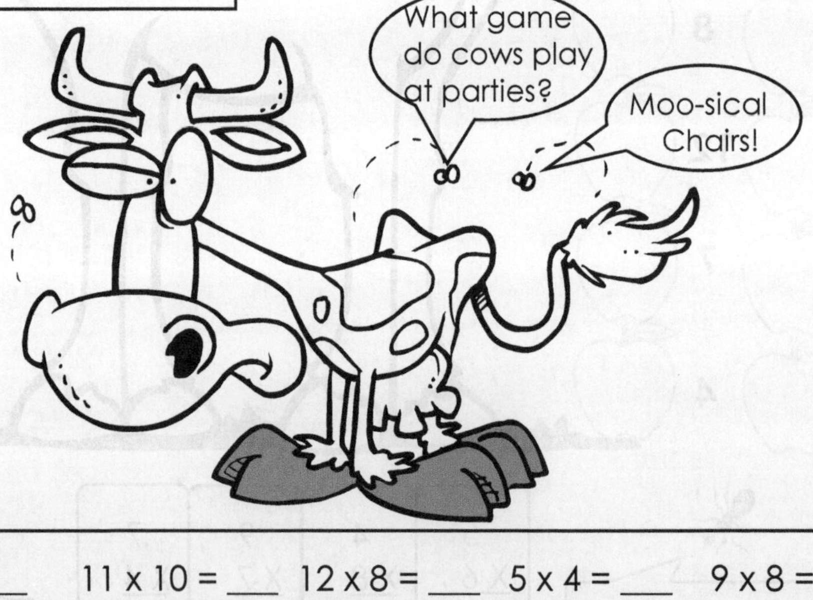

4 x 3 =___	11 x 10 = ___	12 x 8 = ___	5 x 4 = ___	9 x 8 = ___
	12 x 12 =___	4 x 4 = ___	7 x 8 = ___	12 x 9 = ___
	5 x 5 =___	12 x 11 = ___	9 x 6 = ___	3 x 10 = ___
		12 x 7 =___	8 x 2 = ___	5 x 7 = ___

Moo-ve!

38

©Carmel Musumeci
Coroneos Publications

Australian Homeschooling

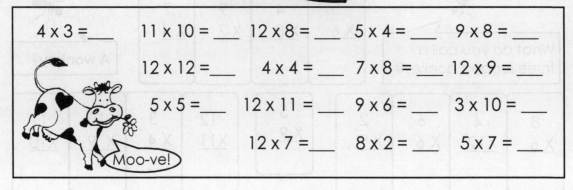

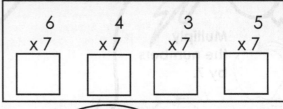

Multiplication by 7

Write out the seven times multiplication table twice.

___ x ___ = 7

___ x ___ = 14

___ x ___ = 21

___ x ___ = 28

___ x ___ = 35

___ x ___ = 42

___ x ___ = 49

___ x ___ = 56

___ x ___ = 63

___ x ___ = 70

___ x ___ = 77

___ x ___ = 84

What's a crocodile's favourite card game?

SNAP!!!

Draw a line from the times table to its matching answer.

6 x 7 ☐	84
3 x 7 ☐	56
12 x 7 ☐	42
4 x 7 ☐	49
8 x 7 ☐	21
2 x 7 ☐	35
7 x 7 ☐	28
5 x 7 ☐	63
10 x 7 ☐	14
9 x 7 ☐	77
11 x 7 ☐	70

39

©Carmel Musumeci
Coroneos Publications

Australian Homeschooling

Multiplication by 7

Write out the seven times multiplication table twice.

3 x 7 =

8 x 7 =

5 x 7 =

11 x 7 =

10 x 7 =

9 x 7 =

4 x 7 =

12 x 7 =

2 x 7 =

7 x 7 =

5 x 7 =

6 x 7 =

8 x 7 =

7 x 7 =

3 x 7 =

4 x 7 =

6 x 7 =

10 x 7 =

12 x 7 =

9 x 7 =

Review of 7

Kangaroos-using-Shampoo
It's time for the Seven Review!

3	6	9	12
x 7	x 7	x 7	x 7
☐	☐	☐	☐
11	7	4	8
x 7	x 7	x 7	x 7
☐	☐	☐	☐

If you know them all, get out those colouring pens for page 4!

4	8	10	11	7	9
x 7	x 7	x 7	x 7	x 7	x 7
☐	☐	☐	☐	☐	☐
6	1	2	5	12	3
x 7	x 7	x 7	x 7	x 7	x 7
☐	☐	☐	☐	☐	☐

7 x 3 = ~~~~~
7 x 5 = ~~~~~
7 x 9 = ~~~~~
7 x 7 = ~~~~~
7 x 11 = ~~~~~
7 x 1 = ~~~~~

7 x 4 = ...
7 x 2 = ...
7 x 6 = ...
7 x 8 = ...
7 x 12 = ...
7 x 6 = ...

2 x 2 = ...
4 x 4 = ...
6 x 6 = ...
8 x 8 = ...
10 x 10 = ...
12 x 12 = ...

The Eleven Times Multiplication Table

11

1 x 11 = 11	7 x 11 = 77
2 x 11 = 22	8 x 11 = 88
3 x 11 = 33	9 x 11 = 99
4 x 11 = 44	10x 11 = 110
5 x 11 = 55	11x 11 = 121
6 x 11 = 66	12x 11 = 132

Write out the eleven times table twice.

You only need to learn one more table! It is 11 x 11 = 121.

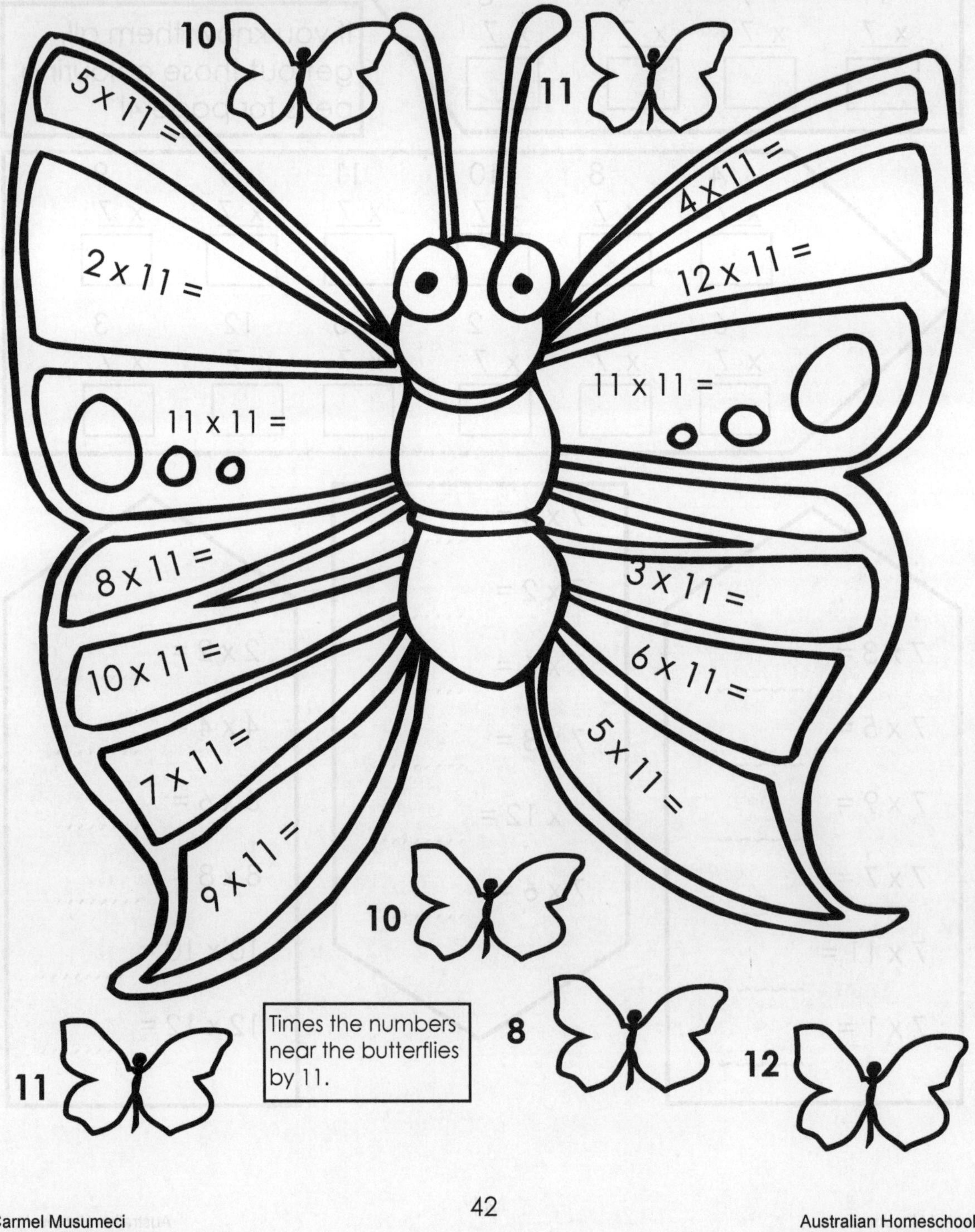
10
11
5 x 11 =
4 x 11 =
2 x 11 =
12 x 11 =
11 x 11 =
11 x 11 =
8 x 11 =
3 x 11 =
10 x 11 =
6 x 11 =
7 x 11 =
5 x 11 =
9 x 11 =
10
8
11
12

Times the numbers near the butterflies by 11.

Multiplication by 11

Write out the eleven times multiplication table twice.

4 x 11 =

8 x 11 =

6 x 11 =

10 x 11 =

9 x 11 =

---

5 x 11 =

12 x 11 =

7 x 11 =

11 x 11 =

---

6 x 11 =

8 x 11 =

12 x 11 =

9 x 11 =

7 x 11 =

10 x 11 =

11 x 11 =

5 x 11 =

7 x 11 =

11 x 11 =

2 x 11 =

12 x 11 =

3 x 11 =

---

6 x 11 =

8 x 11 =

12 x 11 =

9 x 11 =

43

©Carmel Musumeci
Coroneos Publications

Australian Homeschooling

Multiplication by 11

Write out the eleven times multiplication table twice.

11 x 1 = ____	11 x 2 = ____
11 x 3 = ____	11 x 4 = ____
11 x 5 = ____	11 x 6 = ____
11 x 7 = ____	11 x 8 = ____
11 x 9 = ____	11 x10 = ____
11 x11= ____	11 x12 =____

Multiply the number beside the paw prints by 11 and write the answer inside the paw print.

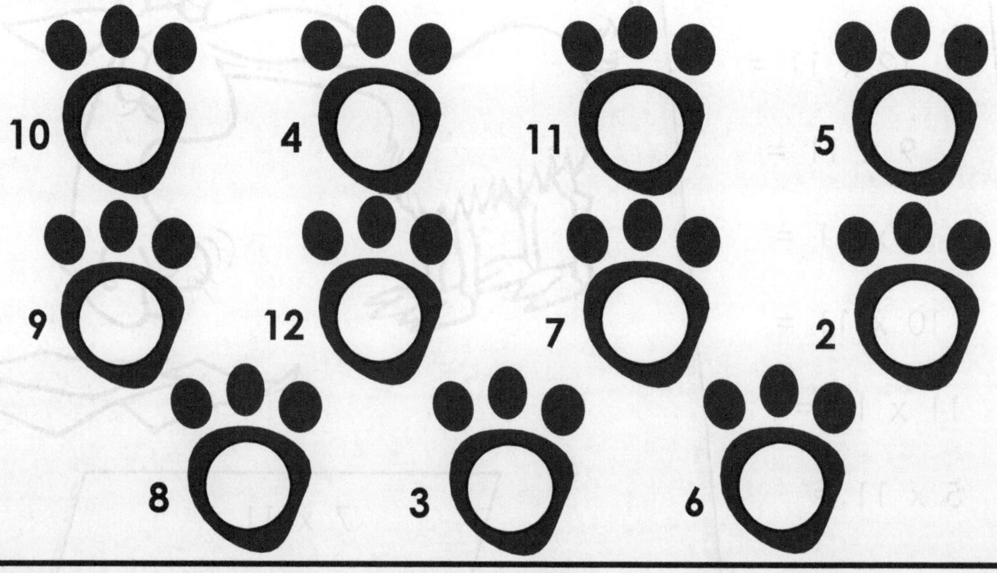

10	4	5	7	11	9	6	12
x 4	x 7	x 8	x 6	x 12	x 9	x 8	x 10

12	8	9	6	7	10
x 9	x 7	x 5	x 12	x 7	x 10

Multiplication by 11

Write out the eleven times multiplication table twice.

2	6	9	10	4	5
x 7	x 7	x 7	x 7	x 7	x 7

7	1	11	3	12	8
x 7	x 7	x 7	x 7	x 7	x 7

5	2	12	8	6	3
x 7	x 7	x 7	x 7	x 7	x 7

1	4	10	5	7	11
x 7	x 7	x 7	x 7	x 7	x 7

2 x 2 = ...	3 x 3 = ...	4 x 5 = ...	4 x 4 = ...	5 x 5 = ...
6 x 7 = ...	9 x 4 = ...	8 x 8 = ...	7 x 5 = ...	5 x 9 = ...
3 x 7 = ...	2 x 12 = ...	3 x 6 = ...	8 x 4 = ...	7 x 9 = ...
12 x 6 = ...	7 x 3 = ...	9 x 6 = ...	6 x 5 = ...	8 x 5 = ...

10 x 11 = ...

8 x 5 = ...

6 x 8 = ...

8 x 8 = ...

7 x 7 = ...

9 x 3 = ...

12 x 4 = ...

3 x 4 = ...

©Carmel Musumeci
Coroneos Publications

Australian Homeschooling

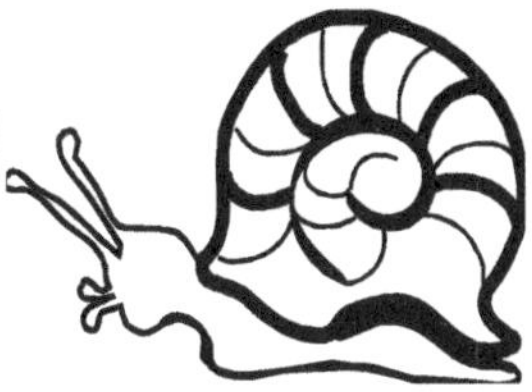

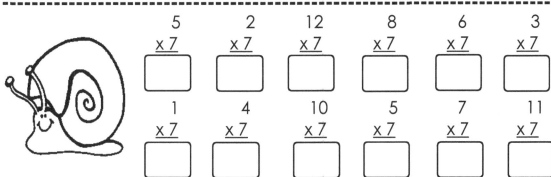

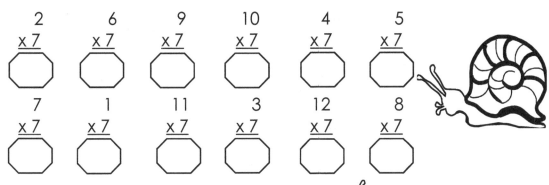

Multiplication by 11

Write out the eleven times multiplication table twice.

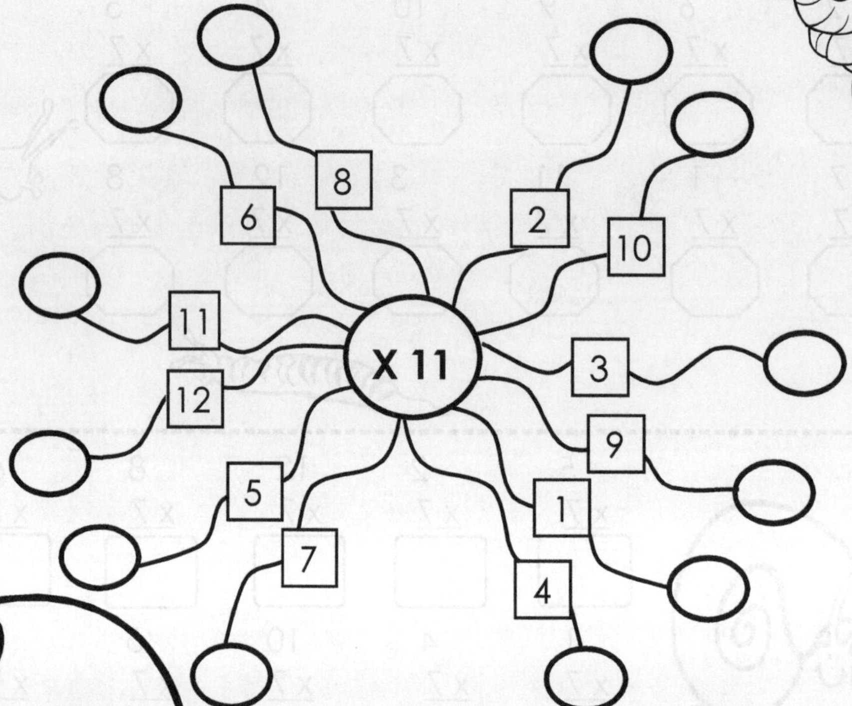

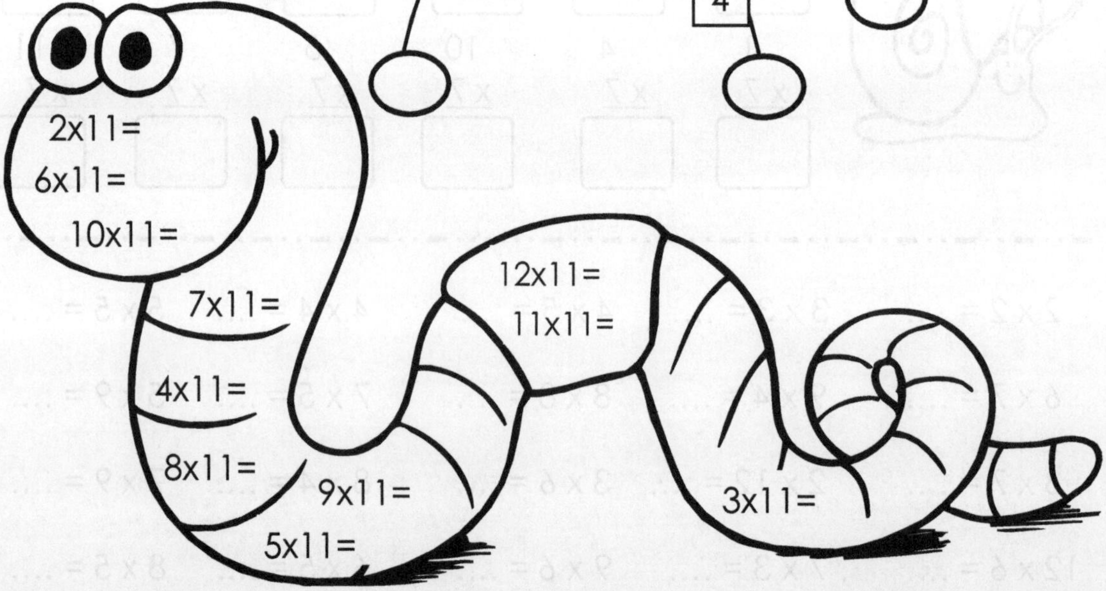

Multiply the number beside the shape by **11**.

Multiplication by 11

Write out the eleven times multiplication table twice.

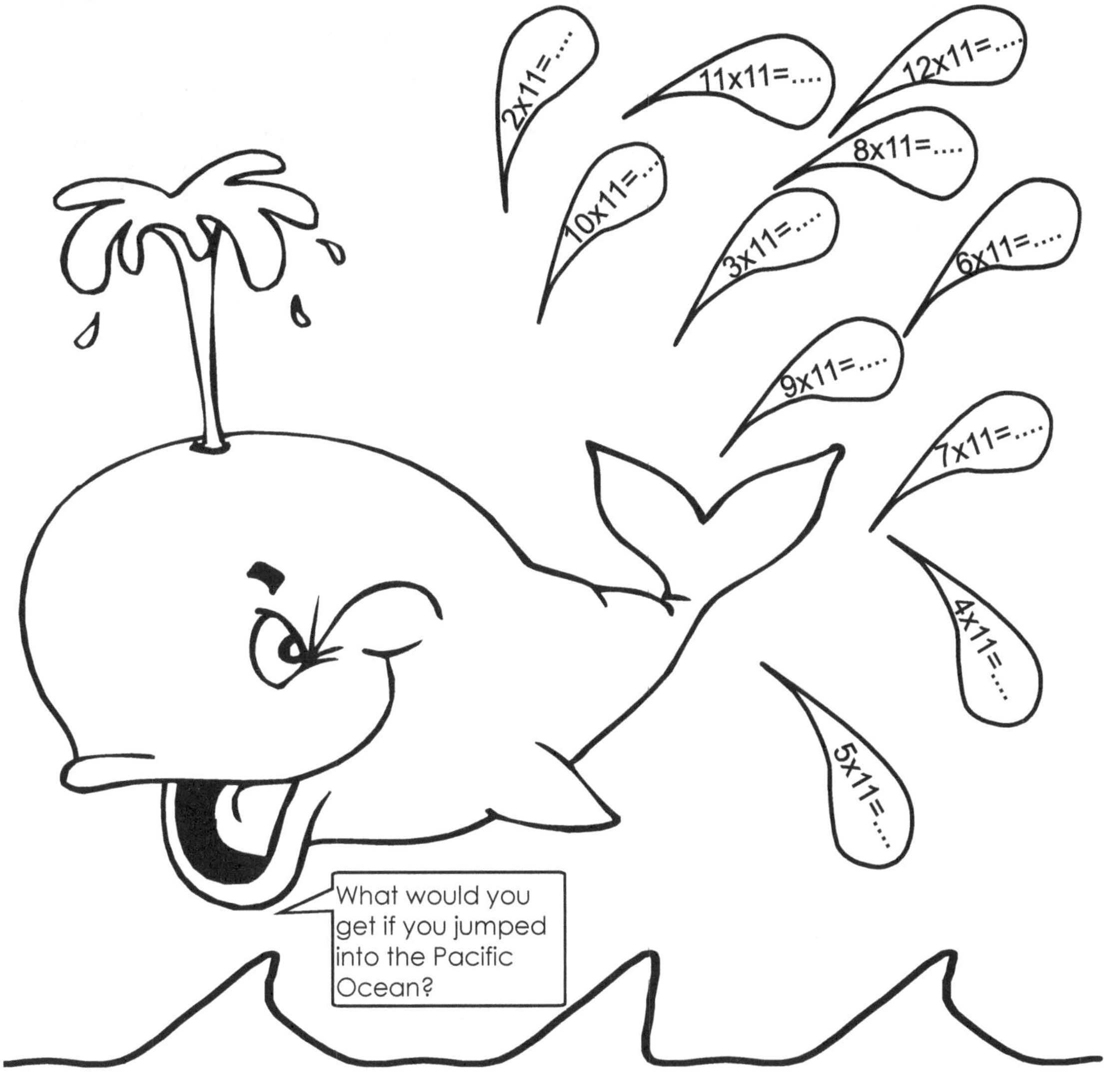

$6 \times 4 =$ _ _ _ $8 \times 6 =$ _ _ _ $7 \times 5 =$ _ _ _ $9 \times 6 =$ _ _ _

$9 \times 7 =$ _ _ _ $4 \times 8 =$ _ _ _ $12 \times 10=$ _ _ _ $7 \times 7 =$ _ _ _

$8 \times 9 =$ _ _ _ $7 \times 6 =$ _ _ _ $3 \times 9 =$ _ _ _ $4 \times 5 =$ _ _ _

$12 \times 12=$ _ _ _ $9 \times 5 =$ _ _ _ $8 \times 7 =$ _ _ _ $8 \times 12=$ _ _ _

$3 \times 8 =$ _ _ _ $6 \times 6 =$ _ _ _ $7 \times 4 =$ _ _ _ $12 \times 9 =$ _ _ _

47

Australian Homeschooling

Multiplication by 11

Write out the eleven times multiplication table twice.

7 x 11 =
8 x 11 =
2 x 11 =
5 x 11 =
10 x 11 =
11 x 11 =
6 x 11 =
4 x 11 =
9 x 11 =
3 x 11 =
11 x 11 =
12 x 11 =

What do you give a sick pig?

Oinkment.

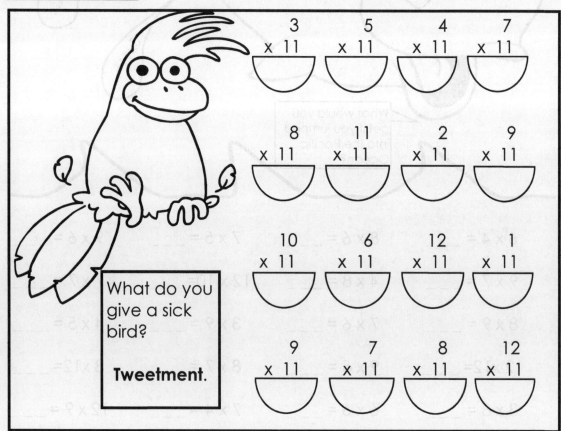

3	5	4	7
x 11	x 11	x 11	x 11
8	11	2	9
x 11	x 11	x 11	x 11
10	6	12	1
x 11	x 11	x 11	x 11
9	7	8	12
x 11	x 11	x 11	x 11

What do you give a sick bird?

Tweetment.

Multiplication by 11

Write out the eleven times multiplication table twice.

☐	5	☐	12	10	☐
x 11	x 11	x 11	x 11	x 11	x 11
44	☐	99	☐	☐	33

6	☐	11	7	☐	☐
x 11	x 11	x 11	x 11	x 11	x 11
☐	88	☐	☐	22	121

- 9 x 5 =....
- 7 x 8 =....
- 6 x 12 =....
- 8 x 9 =....
- 12 x 7 =....
- 5 x 6 =....
- 10 x 10 =....
- 6 x 7 =....
- 8 x 8 =....
- 9 x 7 =....
- 8 x 12 =....
- 7 x 7 =....
- 12 x 9 =....
- 5 x 5 =....
- 8 x 6 =....
- 5 x 12 =....
- 6 x 6 =....
- 11 x 10 =....
- 9 x 9 =....
- 8 x 4 =....
- 9 x 6 =....
- 7 x 12 =....
- 4 x 9 =....
- 8 x 5 =....
- 10 x 12 =....
- 4 x 7 =....
- 4 x 6 =....
- 12 x 12 =....

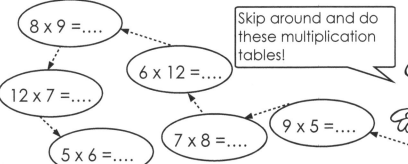

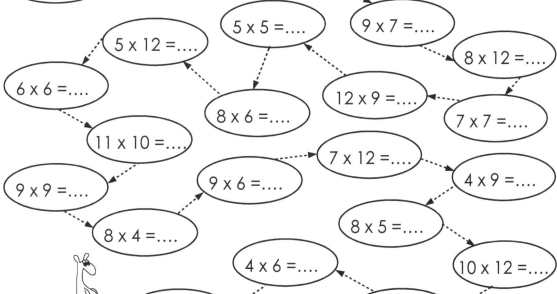

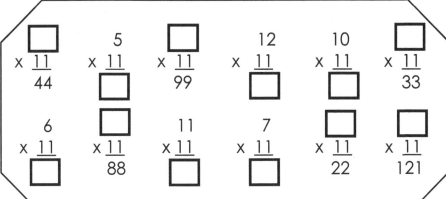

Multiplication by 11

Write out the eleven times multiplication table twice.

11 x11

11 x 3

11 x 8

11 x10

11 x 7

11 x 4

11 x12

11 x 1

11 x 5

11 x 2

11 x 6

11 x11

Elephants don't forget!
They always **remember**!

If you've learnt all of your times tables well - you will always **remember** them!

3 x 4 =	7 x 5 =	8 x 6 =	4 x 9 =	3 x 3 =
7 x 12=	6 x 7 =	11 x 3 =	9 x 3 =	4 x 4 =
8 x 2 =	5 x 9 =	3 x 8 =	10 x 11 =	7 x 9 =
2 x 12 =	8 x 5 =	9 x 2 =	8 x 8 =	6 x 12 =
5 x 5 =	8 x 7 =	11 x 11 =	3 x 2 =	7 x 4 =
4 x 5 =	6 x 3 =	2 x 10 =	3 x 7 =	
9 x 12 =	8 x 11 =	7 x 2 =	9 x 9 =	

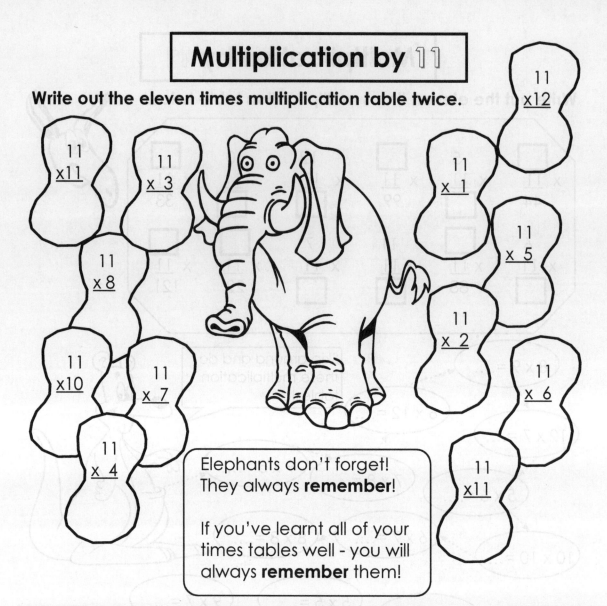

Platypuses-making-a-Hullabaloo,
It's the Last Review for you!

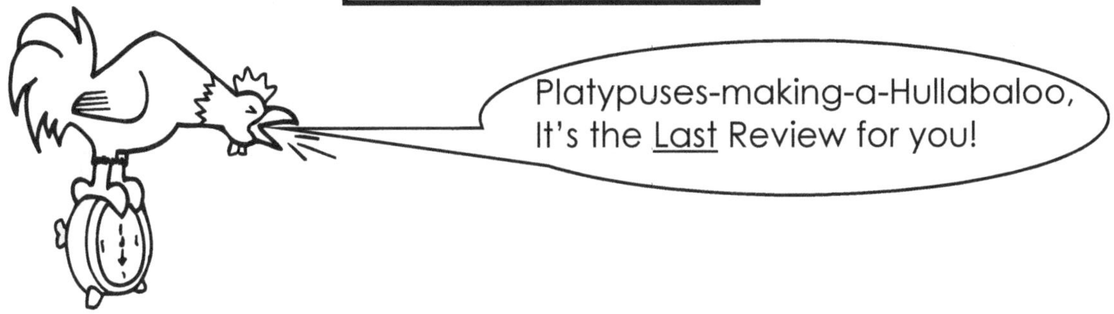

1 x 11 =.... 3 x 11 =.... 7 x 11 =.... 8 x 11 =....

5 x 11 =.... 11 x 11 =.... 10 x 11 =.... 12 x 11 =....

2 x 11 =.... 4 x 11 =.... 6 x 11 =.... 9 x 11 =....

3	7	9	11	10	1
x 11	x 11	x 11	x 11	x 11	x 11

12	4	8	5	6	2
x 11	x 11	x 11	x 11	x 11	x 11

5 x 2 =

7 x 8 =

9 x 9 =

11 x 12 =

4 x 8 =

6 x 6 =

8 x 12 =

4 x 7 =

12 x 6 =

8 x 5 =

6 x 9 =

4 x 6 =

7 x 5 =

3 x 7 =

6 x 8 =

11 x 10 =

7 x 8 =

8 x 8 =

9 x 4 =

5 x 9 =

10 x 7 =

9 x 10 =

6 x 7 =

5 x 10 =

7 x 12 =

11 x 9 =

10 x 12 =

12 x 9 =

Australian Homeschooling

Multiplication Test

3 x 4	7 x 6	4 x 8	9 x 5	10 x 10	5 x 3
6 x 8	2 x 3	11 x 5	8 x 8	4 x 12	12 x 7
2 x 5	6 x 6	7 x 8	10 x 5	5 x 12	8 x 3

9 x 8	12 x 3	3 x 7	4 x 9	8 x 12	10 x 7
3 x 3	8 x 5	6 x 2	5 x 4	10 x 11	7 x 4
2 x 8	6 x 3	10 x 9	7 x 5	2 x 12	4 x 4

11 x 4	9 x 6	7 x 2	8 x 11	6 x 10	9 x 3
10 x 12	2 x 2	5 x 5	6 x 4	11 x 12	10 x 4
6 x 5	7 x 7	4 x 2	11 x 3		

Score: ____ / 52

Coroneos Publications

Multiplication Test

4 x 5	7 x 9	11 x 6	8 x 10	6 x 12	5 x 9
3 x 7	2 x 4	11 x 11	6 x 7	2 x 10	12 x 9
5 x 5	6 x 11	7 x 8	9 x 2	12 x 12	8 x 4
10 x 3	12 x 4	3 x 8	4 x 9	8 x 9	7 x 4
3 x 3	9 x 6	7 x 9	5 x 5	12 x 11	4 x 8
9 x 9	10 x 5	2 x 12	8 x 5	9 x 12	6 x 4
12 x 7	6 x 6	7 x 7	11 x 11	10 x 10	2 x 3
5 x 9	7 x 5	12 x 5	4 x 4	8 x 12	5 x 6
12 x 10	3 x 9	4 x 2	11 x 3		

Score: ____ / 52

Multiplication Test

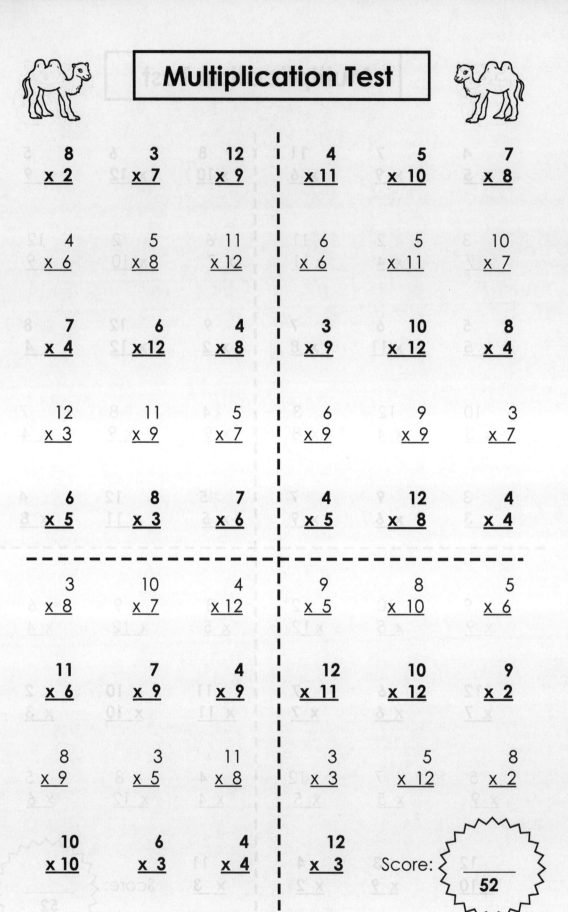

8 x 2	3 x 7	12 x 9	4 x 11	5 x 10	7 x 8
4 x 6	5 x 8	11 x 12	6 x 6	5 x 11	10 x 7
7 x 4	6 x 12	4 x 8	3 x 9	10 x 12	8 x 4
12 x 3	11 x 9	5 x 7	6 x 9	9 x 9	3 x 7
6 x 5	8 x 3	7 x 6	4 x 5	12 x 8	4 x 4
3 x 8	10 x 7	4 x 12	9 x 5	8 x 10	5 x 6
11 x 6	7 x 9	4 x 9	12 x 11	10 x 12	9 x 2
8 x 9	3 x 5	11 x 8	3 x 3	5 x 12	8 x 2
10 x 10	6 x 3	4 x 4	12 x 3	Score: ____ / 52	

Learning Multiplication Ideas

On the following pages are some ideas that you may wish to use to help with learning your multiplication.
Page 60 has another Test, instead of a blank page, for tables to cut out for the Table Match game.

Manipulatives:
Manipulatives can usually be found around your home.
They are things that you may have a lot of that you can use easily to form into groups of things.
A good manipulative is buttons, as are coins and pegs.
When you start learning multiplication, it may help you to form groups of things to show you what multiplication is and how it works.
Basically it is just adding up the same number a certain amount of times. Like 4 x 3, which is 4 + 4 + 4.
So by using buttons you can show 4 groups of 3 is really:

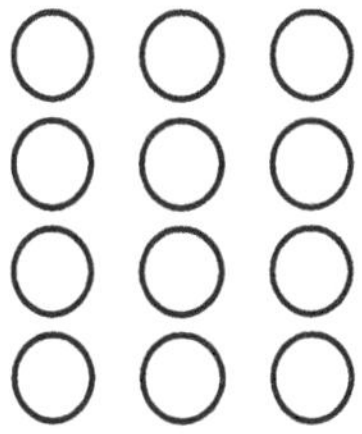

But you can also show that it can be 3 x 4 as well:

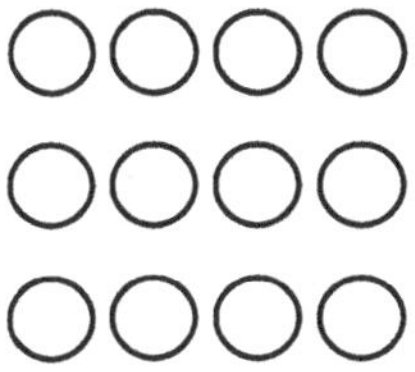

Table Match: Play a game of match by cutting out the tables and their answers (separately) on the next page.
Glue them onto stiff cardboard, then turn them face down and try to match up the table with its answer.
You may wish to also write or print up some of your own of all of the other times tables or perhaps just the ones you know you need to spend more time learning.

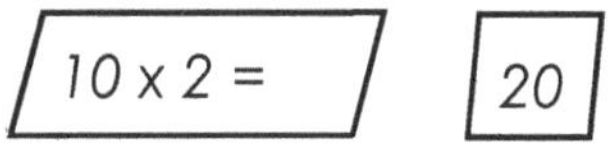

Flashcards:
Make some up as flashcards - get someone to hold them up for you to answer.
How many can you do in 1 minute? Try to get faster!
Put the ones you get correct into one pile and the incorrect into another. Say the ones you got incorrect 5 times each and then get someone to ask you them again.

1 x 2 =	2	7 x 2 =	14
2 x 2 =	4	8 x 2 =	16
3 x 2 =	6	9 x 2 =	18
4 x 2 =	8	10 x 2 =	20
5 x 2 =	10	11 x 2 =	22
6 x 2 =	12	12 x 2 =	24

1 x 3 =	3	7 x 3 =	21
2 x 3 =	6	8 x 3 =	24
3 x 3 =	9	9 x 3 =	27
4 x 3 =	12	10 x 3 =	30
5 x 3 =	15	11 x 3 =	33
6 x 3 =	18	12 x 3 =	36

Multiplication Test

7 x 5	4 x 9	12 x 6	8 x 11	7 x 12	8 x 9
3 x 8	2 x 9	10 x 11	7 x 6	2 x 11	12 x 8
6 x 5	6 x 12	8 x 8	4 x 2	11 x 12	8 x 5
12 x 3	11 x 4	4 x 8	7 x 9	9 x 9	7 x 4
6 x 3	8 x 6	6 x 9	4 x 5	12 x 12	5 x 8
9 x 5	11 x 5	9 x 12	7 x 5	8 x 12	6 x 6
10 x 7	4 x 6	8 x 7	11 x 10	10 x 6	2 x 9
4 x 4	7 x 3	11 x 5	5 x 4	8 x 11	3 x 6
12 x 11	9 x 9	4 x 7	12 x 5	Score:	____ / 52

Learning Multiplication Ideas

You can make up a times table chart for each number and then somewhere, like in your garage, where there is plenty of room, hang it on the wall and skip as you say each table.
This can also be done on a swing too.

Table Catch:
A fun game is to have an adult or older child say a table just before they throw you a large ball, like a basketball. Then, before you catch it, you must say the answer.
As you get better and faster at this, for every correct answer, you step forward, but for every incorrect answer, you step a pace backwards. (It may be a good idea to play this outside.)
You win if you get close enough to touch the thrower.
They win if you get so far away that you miss catching the ball.

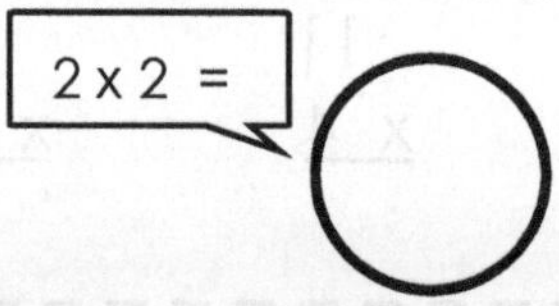

Times Tables D.J.:
Have you got a cassette recorder and a blank cassette?
Record your voice saying the times tables, then play them back to yourself. You can teach your younger brother, sister or friend their times tables too.
Add some music with a beat in the background.
Later you can make tests and say "Twelve times two equals"... and leave time for someone to answer.
A parent or older child can do the recording for you if you prefer.

Picture Multiplying:
By using pictures of things from magazines and old books, you can show a multiplication table.
For example, find several pictures of people and 2 pictures of houses or cars. Or you can draw the house/car.
To show 2 x 3 = 6, glue 3 people on one house or a car and beside them another group of 3 people on the house/car.
Then write the fact underneath.
If you are having trouble with any table, use this idea and hang it somewhere so you can see it and say it during the day.

Learning Multiplication Ideas

2	15		30		54	63		80	
	16	24		42	55		72		90
5		25	32			64		84	
	18			45	56	66		88	
9		28	36	48			77		99

Bingo:

Make up your own Bingo cards. Then your parent can ask times table questions like **3 x 3 =** and if you have the answer, colour it in.

Before you start the game, agree when you will play until, like until all of the numbers in one line are filled in.

Coin Counting:

Using five cent coins, make a group of 12, 5 cent coins and count them, saying the 5 times tables. Do the same with groups of 10 cent coins.

Learning Multiplication Ideas

Uno Maths:

If you have a set of Uno Cards, or even the normal playing cards, remove the cards that don't have numbers, I.e. wild cards or king, queen etc. Then shuffle them and deal them to each player.
Begin with the first player putting down his first two cards and then as fast as possible saying the answer of the two numbers multiplied together. So if he/she puts down 3 and 5, he will say, "15".
If he isn't able to say it quickly enough, the cards go to the other player.
Play then continues with the next player.

5 x 4 = 20

Normal Card Maths:

If your normal playing cards are an old set, perhaps you can make the Queen card = 11 and the King card = 12.
Either write it on the card if they are an old set or try to remember its value and include the King and Queen with the numbers when you play.

Double Domino Dots:

If you have a set of dominoes, you can use them for multiplication games as well.
They are a good way to show you that when you are multiplying a number by two it is the same as doubling that number, like **3 + 3 = 2 x 3** and **4 + 4 = 2 x 4**.

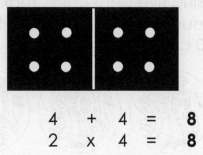

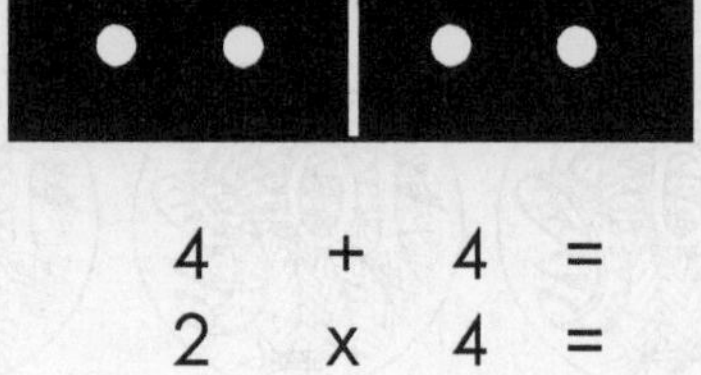

4 + 4 = **8**
2 x 4 = **8**

Answers

Page 4:
12	28	20	44
32	48	8	40
16	36	24	4

8, 3, 9, 2, 7
11, 5, 12, 4, 6
9 x 4 =<u>36</u>, 4 x 4 =<u>16</u>, 7 x 4=<u>28</u>; 11 x 4=<u>44</u>, 6 x 4=<u>24</u>;
5 x 4=<u>20</u>, 8 x 4=<u>32</u>; 10 x 4=<u>40</u>, 12 x 4=<u>48</u>

How fast?
24	24	35	36
48	27	36	72
20	60	24	63
16	40	72	42

Page 5:
yellow=12, green=16, black=20, orange=24, light blue=28, purple=32, pink=36, brown=40, red=44, dark blue=48

Page 6:
8, 24, 16; 44, 12, 28; 20, 32, 48; 36, 4, 40

Elephant's sign:
(v) 36, 16, 28, 48, 20, 40, 32

How fast?
27, 36, 40, 60, 90, 36; 24, 63, 110, 120;
45, 100, 48, 12, 108

Page 7:
16 28 12; 32 20 36
8 40 24; 44 20 48
5x4=<u>20</u>, 4x4=<u>16</u>, 11x4=<u>44</u>, 2x4=<u>8</u>, 10x4=<u>40</u>, 8x4=<u>32</u>
6x4=<u>24</u>, 12x4=<u>48</u>, 3x4=<u>12</u>, 9x4=<u>36</u>, 7x4=<u>28</u>
5, 3; 9, 12; 10, 8; 6, 7; 11

Page 8:
20 28 44; 48 32 24; 36 12 16
12x10=<u>120</u>, 4x3=<u>12</u>, 6x7=<u>42</u>, 7x3=<u>21</u>, 8x5=<u>40</u>,
4x5=<u>20</u>, 9x6=<u>54</u>, 6x5=<u>30</u>, 12x5=<u>60</u>, 5x5=<u>25</u>,
11x10=<u>110</u>, 7x5=<u>35</u>, 9x5=<u>45</u>, 12x6=<u>72</u>, 6x6=<u>36</u>,
9x2=<u>18</u>, 8x2=<u>16</u>, 6x2=<u>12</u>, 7x2=<u>14</u>, 12x5=<u>60</u>,
10x10=<u>100</u>, 8x6=<u>48</u>

Page 9:
8; 20, 32, 24, 44, 28; 16, 40, 12, 36, 48

How fast?
12	18	24	30	36
42	48	54	60	66
72	18	27	36	45
54	63	72	81	90
99	108			

Page 10:
12	20	28	36	44
16	24	32	40	48

24, 40, 12, 20; 16, 36, 8, 44; 28, 32, 48

Page 11:
Left side:
4 8; 12 16; 20 24 28 32; 36 40 44 48

28 12 36; 24 44 32;
16 20 48; 8 40 4;

Page 11 (continued):
Right side:
(v)10 24 54 24 110 36 48 35 27 72 36 42 81
40 16 25 36 9 100 4

Page 12 (Review of 4):
12	28	16	36	40	24
20	48	8	32	4	44

16	24	36	44		
28	44	20	48		
12	4	32	8		
4	40	28	12	20	48
16	32	24	44	8	36

Page 14:
1x8=<u>8</u>, 2x8=16, 3x8=<u>24</u>, 4x8=32, 5x8=<u>40</u>, 6x8=48,
7x8=<u>56</u>, 8x8=64,9x8=<u>72</u>,10x8=80,11x8=<u>88</u>, 12x8=96

Start at top, going round clockwise:
10x8=<u>80</u>, 5x8=<u>40</u>, 8x8=<u>64</u>, 3x8=<u>24</u>, 4x8=<u>32</u>,11x8=<u>88</u>
2x8=<u>16</u>, 6x8=<u>48</u>, 12x8=<u>96</u>, 9x8=<u>72</u>, 1x8=<u>8</u>, 7x8=<u>56</u>

Page 15:
Starting on top, outer side of 8, going clockwise:
4x8=<u>32</u>, 7x8=<u>56</u>, 3x8=<u>24</u>, 12x8=<u>96</u>, 6x8=<u>48</u>, 9x8=<u>72</u>,
11x8=<u>88</u>, 8x8=<u>64</u>, 11x8=<u>88</u>, 4x8=<u>32</u>, 7x8=<u>56</u>,
2x8=<u>16</u>

Inside circles of 8:
6x8=<u>48</u>, 9x8=<u>72</u>, 10x8=<u>80</u>, 5x8=<u>40</u>; 8x8=<u>64</u>, 2x8=<u>16</u>,
12x8=<u>96</u>, 5x8=<u>40</u>, 3x8=<u>24</u>
10	18	16	45	30
35	48	36	90	55
60	12	12	36	

Page 16:
10x8=<u>80</u>, 2x8=<u>16</u>, 4x8=<u>32</u>, 3x8=<u>24</u>, 5x8=<u>40</u>,
10x8=<u>80</u>, 8x8=<u>64</u>, 6x8=<u>48</u>, 9x8=<u>72</u>, 4x8=<u>32</u>,
11x8=<u>88</u>, 2x8=<u>16</u>, 9x8=<u>72</u>, 12x8=<u>96</u>, 5x8=<u>40</u>,
3x8=<u>24</u>, 9x8=<u>72</u>, 10x8=<u>80</u>, 7x8=<u>56</u>, 9x8=<u>72</u>,
11x8=<u>88</u>, 6x8=<u>48</u>, 12x8=<u>96</u>, 7x8=<u>56</u>, 4x8=<u>32</u>,
3x8=<u>24</u>, 6x8=<u>48</u>, 8x8=<u>64</u>, 6x8=<u>48</u>, 11x8=<u>88</u>, 7x8=<u>56</u>
24	35	24	24	100
54	33	16	48	28
15	60	110	32	30
18	42	45	36	72

Page 17:(follow arrows)
★ 48 88 8 80 72 64 16 32
56 24 40 96
32	48	72	88
56	88	40	96
24	8	64	16

Left Arrow: (v) 30 50; 40 60; 20 80 100 110 120
Right Arrow:(v)90 108 81 99 72; 18 45; 36 27; 54

Page 18:
1x8=<u>8</u>, 10x8=<u>80</u>, 5x8=<u>40</u>, 6x8=<u>48</u>, 7x8=<u>56</u>, 5x8=<u>40</u>,
2x8=<u>16</u>, 9x8=<u>72</u>, 12x8=<u>96</u>, 8x8=<u>64</u>, 1x8=<u>8</u>, 8x8=<u>64</u>,
11x8=<u>88</u>, 4x8=<u>32</u>, 6x8=<u>48</u>, 4x8=<u>32</u>, 3x8=<u>24</u>,
12x8=<u>96</u>, 9x8=<u>72</u>, 10x8=<u>80</u>, 2x8=<u>16</u>, 7x8=<u>56</u>,
11x8=<u>88</u>, 3x8=<u>24</u>

©Carmel Musumeci
Coroneos Publications

Australian Homeschooling

Answers

Page 18 (continued):
1 10 4
3 8 5
6 7 9
11 12 7
9 2 3
Page 19: (start at top of horseshoe, going down vertically in 3 columns)
16, 48, 24, 96, 40, 64, 48, 88, 80, 56, 16;
80, 64, 72;
40, 16, 88, 24, 80, 48, 96, 72, 32, 56
5x5=25, 11x5=55, 3x5=15, 6x5=30, 9x5=45,10x5=50
4x5=20, 7x5=35, 2x5=10, 12x5=60
Page 20:
4x8=32, 5x8=40, 11x8=88, 2x8=16, 10x8=80;
6x8=48, 8x8=64, 9x8=72, 12x8=96, 4x8=32;
12x8=96, 5x8=40, 7x8=56, 4x8=32, 8x8=64, 3x8=24;
11x8=88, 6x8=48, 9x8=72, 10x8=80, 7x8=56
15, 21, 33, 12, 24
18, 36, 30, 6, 27
9, 24, 18, 21, 33
27, 30, 15, 36, 9
12, 6, 18, 24, 15
Page 21:
48, 72, 64, 56
24 88 48
80 56 32
96 40 72
64 8 16
88, 32, 80; 24, 40, 96
4 10 20 16 22 12
8 24 14 6 2 18
10, 16, 20, 18, 22,
6, 14, 2, 24, 4,
42, 110, 25, 48, 48
Page 22 (Review of 8):
40 64 24 72 80 56
88 32 40 96 16 8
10x8=80, 3x8=24; 6x8=48, 12x8=96, 4x8=32,
8x8=64, 5x8=40, 7x8=56; 3x8=24, 9x8=72, 12x8=96,
9x8=72 11x8=88; 5x8=40, 10x8=80, 1x8=8, 8x8=64,
2x8=16; 2x8=16, 7x8=56, 6x8=48, 11x8=88, 4x8=32
Page 23:
Left Column: (v)12, 24, 36, 48, 60, 72, 84, 96, 108, 120, 132, 144
Right Column: (v) 36, 108, 24, 120, 48, 96, 132, 60, 144, 12, 84, 72
Page 24:
l=36, r=96, h=48, w=108, e=60, m=120, o=72, t=132, i=84, s=144 Sit somewhere else!
60, 84, 132, 120, 48, 72, 96, 36, 144, 108, 24
Page 25:
36, 84,72;48;120; 24,132; 96,108,144,60;144,132; 84
Top of Rhino:
99 35 12 32 36 80 60 28 25 42;
45 24 72 16 120; 110 56 24 15

Page 26:
4x12=48,12x12=144; 9x12=108,10x12=120;
8x12= 96; 3x12=36, 5x12=60; 11x12=132;
4x12=48, 7x12=84, 6x12=72; 8x12=96, 10x12=120,
12x12=144; 9x12=108, 11x12=132, 7x12=84
16 24 36 40 8 20
44 4 28 12 48 32
Page 27:
144 132 120 108 96 84
72 60 48 36 24 12
120 144; 132 108
36 96 60 144 84 24
48 120 12 108 72 132
3x4=12,9x2=18,7x5=35,10x10=100;6x7=42,9x6=54,
10x8=80; 5x12=60, 4x8=32, 7x9=63, 11x9=99;
9x4=36, 12x6=72, 7x8=56, 10x11=110; 9x9=81,
8x8=64, 7x7=49; 6x5=30, 12x3=36, 4x7=28, 6x7=42
Page 28:
8 3 12; 9 10 1; 5 6 7; 2 11 4
48, 132, 60, 120; 96, 108, 36, 72; 84, 144, 108,144
32 30 35 22 20 24 54 24
16 48 20 24
36 72 45 16
20 42 40 14
Page 29:
Hare: 16, 72; 48, 56; 132, 60; 72, 132; 12, 96; 36, 120; 84, 144, 40, 72
Tortoise: 48, 24; 60, 108; 8, 84; 96, 144; 24, 80; 32, 64; 84, 72, 40, 88
Page 30:
108 60; 48 120; 84 60; 132 36; 108 96;
108 96; 72 144; 144 84; 84 72; 48 120
8 16 20 28 24
36 32 40 48 44
16 32 40 56 48
72 64 80 96 88
Page 31:
60 36 96 120 24 84; 72 108 144; 48 132;
96 84 144 108 72 48
6 8 4 7
12 10 5 6
11 12 9 7
Page 32 (Review of 12):
36 144; 72 120; 48 60; 96 84 72 108;
132 24 144 72; 12 108 132 96
1st column of pentagons:
(v) 36, 36, 21; 32, 27, 42; 64, 54, 20
2nd column of pentagons:
(v) 40, 22, 60; 72, 25, 36; 108, 48, 60
3rd column of pentagons:
(v) 96, 16, 45; 9, 55, 45; 8, 110, 24
4th column of pentagons:
(v) 30, 15, 28; 20, 18, 12; 35, 88, 60
5th column of pentagons:
(v) 56, 81, 66; 100, 42, 4; 6, 99, 50

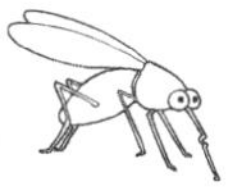

Answers

Page 34:

7	14	21
28	35	42
49	56	63
70	77	84

3	4	7	6	9	6	10	4
8	8	7	12	9	8	4	9

Page 35:

14	42	63	70	28
49	7	77	21	84
21	56	35	84	70
42	49	28	63	84

5, 12, 7, 11
1, 3, 10, 8
4, 2, 9, 6

How fast?

32	27	60	72
42	110	24	35
54	96	56	30
108	33	48	64

Page 36:
Column 1:
(v) 14, 42, 77, 28, 63, 21, 70, 35, 49, 7, 84, 28, 56, 35, 77, 63
Column 2:
(v) 49, 21, 28, 56, 63, 77, 14, 84, 70, 35, 42, 84, 49
Column 3:
35 64; 72 27; 110 36; 42 96; 81 48

Page 37:

28	14	56	35
49	21	77	63
77	42	28	84
56	49	70	
63	42		

6x7=$\underline{42}$, 9x7=$\underline{63}$, 8x7=$\underline{56}$, 5x7=$\underline{35}$, 12x7=$\underline{84}$,11x7=$\underline{77}$
7x5=$\underline{35}$, 10x7=$\underline{70}$, 4x7=$\underline{28}$

30	32	63	28				
48	48	36	18	45	132	12	90	110

Page 38:
Box 1: (v) 35 28 56 21 63 14 49 42
Box 2: (v) 84 42 77 35 7 70 56 49
Box 3: (v) 14 35 77 70 28 63 49 42 21
Box 4: (v) 3 11 5 12 9 4 8 7
Box 5: (v) 56, 49, 84, 63
Box 6: 42, 28, 21, 35
Moo-ve:

12	110	96	20	72
144	16	56	84
25	132	54	30
84	16	35	

Page 39:
Column 1:
(v) $\underline{1 \times 7}$ = 7; $\underline{2 \times 7}$ = 14; $\underline{3 \times 7}$ = 21; $\underline{4 \times 7}$ = 28; $\underline{5 \times 7}$ = 35; $\underline{6 \times 7}$ = 42

Page 39 (continued):
Column 2:
(v) $\underline{7 \times 7}$ = 49; $\underline{8 \times 7}$ = 56; $\underline{9 \times 7}$ = 63; $\underline{10 \times 7}$ = 70; $\underline{11 \times 7}$ = 77; $\underline{12 \times 7}$ = 84
Draw a line:
6 x 7 = $\underline{42}$, 3 x 7 = $\underline{21}$, 12 x 7 = $\underline{84}$, 4 x 7 = $\underline{28}$,
8 x 7 = $\underline{56}$, 2 x 7 = $\underline{14}$, 7 x 7 = $\underline{49}$, 5 x 7 = $\underline{35}$,
10 x 7 = $\underline{70}$, 9 x 7 = $\underline{63}$, 11 x 7 = $\underline{77}$

Page 40:
3 x 7 = $\underline{21}$; 5 x 7 = $\underline{35}$; 8 x 7 = $\underline{56}$; 9 x 7 = $\underline{63}$;
11 x 7 = $\underline{77}$; 10 x 7 = $\underline{70}$; 4 x 7 = $\underline{28}$;
2 x 7 = $\underline{14}$; 12 x 7 = $\underline{84}$; 5 x 7 = $\underline{35}$; 7 x 7 = $\underline{49}$;
6 x 7 = $\underline{42}$; 8 x 7 = $\underline{56}$; 7 x 7 = $\underline{49}$; 4 x 7 = $\underline{28}$;
3 x 7 = $\underline{21}$; 6 x 7 = $\underline{42}$; 12 x 7 = $\underline{84}$; 10 x 7 = $\underline{70}$;
9 x 7 = $\underline{63}$

Page 41 (Review of 7):

21	42	63	84		
77	49	28	56		
28	56	70	77	49	63
42	7	14	35	84	21

Column 1:
(v) 21 35 63 49 77 7
Column 2:
(v) 28 14 42 56 84 42
Column 3:
(v) 16 36 64 100 144

Page 42 (Little Butterflies):
10x11=$\underline{110}$, 11x11=$\underline{121}$, 11x11=$\underline{121}$, 10x11=$\underline{110}$,
8x11=$\underline{88}$, 12x11=$\underline{132}$
Left Wing:
(v) 55 22 121 88 110 77 99
Right Wing:
(v) 44 132 121 33 66 55

Page 43:
Box 1 (v) 44 88 66 110 99
Box 2 (v) 55 132 77 121
Box 3 (v) 66 88 132 99 77 110 121 55
Box 4 (v) 66 88 132 99
Box 5 (v) 77 121 22 132 33

Page 44:
11, 22; 33, 44; 55, 66; 77, 88; 99, 110; 121, 132
10x11=$\underline{110}$, 4x11=$\underline{44}$,11x11=$\underline{121}$, 5x11=$\underline{55}$; 9x11=$\underline{99}$
12x11=$\underline{132}$, 7x11=$\underline{77}$, 2x11=$\underline{22}$; 8x11=$\underline{88}$, 3x11=$\underline{33}$
6x11= 66

40	28	40	42	132	81	48	120
108	56	45	72	49	100	

Page 45:

14	42	63	70	28	35
49	7	77	21	84	56
35	14	84	56	42	21
7	28	70	35	49	77

4, 9, 20, 16, 25,
42, 36, 64, 35, 45,
21, 24, 18, 32, 63,
72, 21, 54, 30, 40

©Carmel Musumeci
Coroneos Publications

Australian Homeschooling

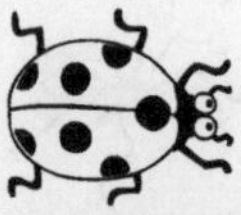

Answers

Page 45 (continued):
Left: (v) 110, 40, 48, 64
Right: (v) 49, 27, 48, 12

Page 46: (starting top right, going clockwise)
11 x 2= 22, 11 x 10 = 110, 11 x 3 = 33, 11 x 9 = 99, 11 x 1 = 11, 11 x 4 = 44, 11 x 7 = 77, 11 x 5 = 55, 11 x 12 = 132, 11 x 11 = 121, 11 x 6 = 66,11 x 8 = 88

22 66 110 77 44 88 55 99
132 121 33

5x11=55, 8x11=88, 10x11=110, 12x11=132,
7x11=77 9x11=99, 11x11=121, 6x11=66

Page 47:
2 x 11=22, 11 x 11=121, 12 x 11=132, 10 x 11=110,
3 x 11=33, 8 x 11=88, 9 x 11=99, 6 x 11=66,
7 x 11=77, 4 x 11=44, 5 x 11=55

24 48 35 54
63 32 120 49
72 42 27 20
144 45 56 96
24 36 28 108

Page 48:
(v) 5 x 11=55, 11 x 11=121, 9 x 11=99, 3 x 11=33,
12 x 11=132; 7 x 11=77, 2 x 11=22, 10 x 11=110,
6 x 11=66; 8 x 11=88, 4 x 11=44, 11 x 11 = 121

33 55 44 77
88 121 22 99
110 66 132 11
99 77 88 132

Page 49:
4, 55, 9, 132, 110, 3
66, 8, 121, 77, 2, 11
(starting at pouch) 45 56 72 72 84 30 100 42
64 63 96 49 108 25 48 60 36 110 81 32 54
84 36 40 120 28 24 144

Page 50:
Left Peanuts:
(v) 121 33 88 110 77 44
Right Peanuts:
(v) 132 11 55 22 66 121

12 35 48 36 9
84 42 33 27 16
16 45 24 110 63
24 40 18 64 72
25 56 121 6 28
20 18 20 21
108 88 14 81

Page 51 (Review of 11):
11 33 77 88
55 121 110 132
22 44 66 99

33 77 99 121 110 11
132 44 88 55 66 22

Page 51 (continued):
10 28 48 90
56 72 110 42
81 40 56 50
132 54 64 84
32 24 36 99
36 35 45 120
96 21 70 108

Page 52 Multiplication test:
12 42 32 45 100 15
48 6 55 64 48 84
10 36 56 50 60 24

72 36 21 36 96 70
9 40 12 20 110 28
16 18 90 35 24 16

44 54 14 88 60 27
120 4 25 24 132 40
30 49 8 33

Page 53 Multiplication test:
20 63 66; 80 72 45
21 8 121; 42 20 108
25 66 56; 18 144 32
30 48 24; 36 72 28
9 54 63; 25 132 32

81 50 24; 40 108 24
84 36 49 ; 121 100 6
45 35 60; 16 96 30
120 27 8; 33

Page 54: Multiplication test
16 21 108; 44 50 56
24 40 132; 36 55 70
28 72 32; 27 120 32
36 99 35; 54 81 21
30 24 42; 20 96 16

24 70 48; 45 80 30
66 63 36; 132 120 18
72 15 88; 9 60 16
100 18 16; 36

Page 57: Multiplication test
35 36 72; 88 84 72
24 18 110; 42 22 96
30 72 64; 8 132 40
36 44 32; 63 81 28

18 48 54; 20 144 40
45 55 108; 35 96 36
70 24 56; 110 60 18
16 21 55; 20 88 18
132 81 28; 60